Planning the Urban Region

T0248006

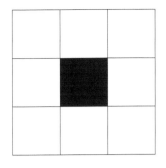

Planning the Urban Region

A Comparative Study of Policies and Organizations

PETER SELF

The University of Alabama Press

Tuscaloosa

The University of Alabama Press
Tuscaloosa, Alabama 35487-0380
uapress.ua.edu

Typeface: Avenir

The graphic used on the title page and the chapter openings is an
adaptation of the planning logo of the city of New Haven, Connecticut,
designed originally by Norman Ives. The logo depicts the 9 square blocks of
the original city.\

Book designed by Anna F. Jacobs

Paperback ISBN: 978-0-8173-5943-0

Cataloging-in-Publication data is available from the Library of Congress.
ISBN 0-8173-0089-0 (cloth)

Contents

Preface

This book is based on a series of lectures given at The University of Alabama in October 1978. The lectures have been extensively revised and expanded.

My focus is the urban region as "a political and organizational crossroads." The first chapter discusses the scope of planning in large urban regions generally. There follow three chapters dealing with the planning systems and policies of three types of organization: large city governments, metro authorities, and central governments. The last chapter considers the possibilities of more comprehensive planning for urban regions and the prospects for institutional reform.

The book is comparative in a selective way. The main aim is not to compare systematically different national systems of urban planning but to illustrate the achievements and problems of different organizations and types of policy. Metro schemes, for example, are illustrated with examples from London, Toronto, and Stockholm. An obvious danger of this approach is that of underplaying the significance of national differences. Much attention has been paid to national differences, however, and little has been given to the common problems of organizations such as cities, metro authorities, or central governments striving to develop suitable regional organizations and policies. This book attempts to fill this gap within a general framework of the aims of planning.

I also introduce national comparisons at several points, particularly with respect to British and American policies. Within Europe the main focus is on Britain, but in addition I take examples from France, Sweden, and other countries. It may legitimately be objected that this comparative material is uneven, but again, I am not attempting a balanced international comparison. I am, however, trying to show how urban planning is dealt with in different political systems, and chapter 4, for example, distinguishes the issues which arise in unitary and federal systems and introduces some Australian material.

The importance of the subject needs little demonstration. When I prepared the first edition of my book *Cities in Flood: The Problems of Urban Growth* (London: Faber & Faber, 1957), publishers opined that no one would read it, because in England, at any rate, people only read about the countryside. Today a book on cities appears virtually every day, and presumably these books are read. The problems of the "urban region" are more than those of the city writ large or of urban sprawl and spread. They include the social effects of highly specialized and differentiated land uses and housing markets, the conflicts between localized communities and an overall metropolitan viewpoint, and the extent of environmental inequalities. The attempts and capacities of governmental systems to handle issues of this kind form the important subject with which this book is concerned.

I was honored to speak in the distinguished series of annual lectures sponsored by the Bureau of Public Administration at the University of Alabama. My thanks for a most interesting and hospitable occasion go to my hosts there and especially to James Thomas and Coleman Ransome. I also warmly thank George Jones, James Sharpe, and John Stewart for many helpful comments on several chapters, although naturally they are not responsible for the results. I am grateful to the Australian National University, Research School of Social Sciences, for a visiting fellowship which facilitated the completion of this book. My warm thanks go to Ann Kennedy and Sandra Self for typing several versions of the manuscript quickly and accurately.

Canberra, March 1981

Planning the Urban Region

1: The Urban Region and Planning Theories

The Urban Region

Many books have been written about the growth and characteristics of large urban regions in modern Western societies. It is not necessary to repeat the analysis here. Rather, this chapter will be concerned with the purposes and rationale of modern urban planning, the meaning and nature of planning itself, and the political and organizational conditions of effective planning. At the outset a few preliminary remarks are necessary about the character of urban regions, as viewed from a standpoint of government interventions and plans.

Modern Western urbanization has proceeded through a process of pull-push, or concentration-diffusion. Large urban areas developed to exploit the economic and social gains of location at nodal points and the economies of scale and markets. Subsequently they diffused and sprawled over ever-widening areas, through processes of urban dispersal and fresh accretions.

Dense concentrations of population grew up in the age of coal and of water and transport. Progressive dispersal came with the impact of mass transit, the car and the truck, and electric power. Environmental factors influenced the dispersal of residences, and economic factors (such as the importance of road transport, the advantages of more spacious and cheaper sites, and the spread of the labor force) influenced the diffusion of manufacturing and routine office operations. These developments need not be pictured as the product of inexorable laws of economic development, since they were also much affected by the distribution of economic and political power. Still, whatever explanations are offered, the trends have been similar in most societies.

The results of the process have included: steady decline in the population of inner urban areas; flattening of densities across broad urban zones; rapid suburban and exurban growth; and rapid *total* growth of major urbanized areas. Traditional concepts of an urban place, as used (for example) for census purposes, need drastic revision when much of the population concentrates in urban areas of more than a million each. By 1970 the proportion of national population in the units formed by such areas was about 40 percent each in the United States, the United Kingdom, and Australia, and the numbers of these units were thirty-one, eight, and two, respectively. But the population in these big urban areas has continually spread farther and thereby invalidated census boundaries. For example, in the United States between 1950 and 1970, the population density within urban areas fell from 5,408 to 3,376 per square mile and within central cities from 7,786 to 4,463.[1]

It is sometimes said that the character of urbanization is changing so radically that the traditional concept of a city or even of a "city region," with its city-suburban and core-periphery patterns, will soon be obsolete. There will no longer be cities but only vast, diffused zones of human activity, conceived as expanding until they almost cover the globe, rather like a gaseous cloud.

Certainly in physical terms urbanization is likely to become still more diffused. Because of their rapid development under the economic conditions of the late nineteenth century, the older metropolitan areas possess large dense urban cores which are still dispersing population and economic activities. By contrast, modern cities "start suburban" to a great extent because of the reduced technological and economic rationale for dense concentrations.

Again, the removal of some of the original causes of urban concentration and the greater freedom of location which now exists for both firms and individuals mean that many advantages of urban concentration are now possible within smaller units. Consequently there may in the future be many more zones of urbanization but relatively fewer giant urban regions. Already the largest multimillion metropolitan units are in general growing less rapidly than those around the 1 million to 2 million mark. The total number of major urbanized areas is growing rapidly, as is the area encompassed by almost every such unit, whatever tests of commuting data or land use data or indexes of economic and social interaction are applied.[2]

It also seems that some reversal of traditional migration from rural to urbanized zones may now be occurring. Such a trend shows mildly for the United States in recent surveys, although one explanation is a still wider expansion of urban commuting beyond the metropolitan area boundaries. Also, some relatively rural and small town zones in the South and elsewhere (such as the Tennessee Valley and the Ozarks) are exhibiting a quite remarkable growth of manufacturing employment. This may be the wave of the future, but at present most rural areas decline or stagnate, and population in all countries is strongly concentrated within certain heavily urbanized regions.[3]

In some people's view, urban structure will be much affected by microchip technology. Easy and instant communication will reduce the functions of city centers, and these centers may in any case be located on greenfield sites instead of embedded within a compacted urban mass. The great world centers of Paris, London, or New York may become historical curiosities, enjoying (as they already do) a vast tourist trade. Individuals and firms will utilize their greater technological freedom of location to combine spacious local surroundings with mobility when required across vast lightly urbanized zones.

But these predictions may also be false in many respects. The physical form of a city as traditionally understood is linked to a discernible pattern of centers and subcenters. Meeting places for a variety of purposes are still likely to be wanted, even in a microchip age. There may be strong reasons connected with transportation efficiency, energy costs, and land conservation for keeping such a pattern, even if (as is quite possible) main centers become detached from their traditional proximity to dense populations.

There are also social and political reasons for drawing the same conclusion. Melvin Webber's concept of the "nonplace urban realm" aroused interest in the 1960s as a description or prediction of a highly mobile urban society where individual preferences had free rein, access costs were minimal, social groupings were functional or optional, and localized community ties counted for almost nothing.[4] Today in the wake of energy crises and racial and social conflicts, such opinions seem less plausible. Access costs were never in fact a negligible factor save to the very affluent. Local community ties are being rediscovered sometimes as a matter of taste but also for the political and economic protection afforded by neighborhood pressure groups and by an "informal economy" in time of depression. It may be that civic loyalties and central meeting grounds will also become more important.

How are we to define "urban region" for the purposes of this book? First, we are concerned here specifically with *large* urban regions, those of 1 million persons or more. More specifically we are concerned with the planning systems of urban regions, and examples are chosen for their relevance to this objective. Second, it is obviously difficult to set geographic limits to our concept of the "urban region," but one consideration is important—namely that effective planning needs in some measure to embrace the urban frontiers as well as the urban core. The forces already discussed are continuously reducing population within urban cores and producing rapid growth in peripheral areas. Planners have to look beyond the urban fence not only for the sites of new development but also for many facilities required for the urban complex as a whole, such as land reserves for recreational, agricultural, and other purposes; water supplies; airports; and many other facilities. The transportation framework needs to comprise and serve areas of growth as well as static or declining zones. The same point applies to measures of pollution control. Equally there is interdependence in terms of social and fiscal policies, since urban growth policy should attempt to help with deprivation in the inner city as well as providing a good environment and facilities for residents in new areas. These inter-dependencies are a fact of life, whether or not public planning con-sciously copes with them, and if it does not, the results seem likely to be unnecessary inefficiencies as well as increasing environmental inequali-ties.

The meaning and scale of "urban region" depends to some extent upon whether and how it is planned. For example, a plan which looks well ahead, which reserves substantial zones of green space for recrea-tion or agriculture, which pushes out the poles of growth through the designation of new towns or other nucleated settlements, and which envisages major developments in transportation and other infrastructure will inevitably comprehend a much wider area than a plan which is incremental and conservative over its assumptions or intentions about urbanization.

It follows that no final definition can be offered of the urban region we have in mind. City boundaries are usually and obviously inadequate for the purpose, and the same applies, though less obviously, to some of the metro schemes discussed in the third chapter. Statistical definitions such as the standard metropolitan statistical area (SMSA) of the United States or the British "conurbation" are more helpful but do not allow for future growth until it occurs. Indeed, such units are now often areas of overall population decline. They will not do for planning purposes, for which a more helpful concept is the "daily urban system" which com-prehends the pattern of daily commuting into some major labor market zone.

Here we have the concept which seventy years ago underlay H. G. Wells's vision of the regional city of the future, a great transporta-tion-linked network which in the case of southeast England extended even in Wells's time well over fifty miles from the center of London in certain directions. But there are difficulties also with this definition. Commuting is defined more by time than by distance zones and in-cludes distant settlements which may have rather little relevance for planning the urban complex. Increasing use of cars and declining public transport have, it is true, changed the impact of commuting and in some cases have actually shrunk the commutershed since Wells's

time, although elsewhere new inventions such as high-speed trains
have enlarged it. Trains can travel much faster than cars (and airplanes,
of course, still faster), but use of the car spreads the commutershed into
areas between the major transportation routes. Commuting, however, is
only one relevant factor for planning policies, albeit an important one,
and it may and perhaps should be a major purpose of planning to
reduce the pressures or incentives for long-distance commuting.[5]

Therefore "urban region"[6] has to be defined, for our purposes, by
reference to the case for some degree of comprehensive planning.
What exactly is this case? It will be elaborated as we proceed, but three
aims of such planning can be briefly listed:
1. The integration and coordination of the three major determinants of
   urbanization patterns: the location of residences, the location of
   employment and major service facilities, and the transportation network.
2. The planning and conservation of the resource base of the urban
   region, including land, water, air, and energy.
3. The improvement of the urban environment, and the allocation of
   environmental costs and benefits, across a zone of high inter-
   dependencies in terms of locational possibilities and relationships.
For the first purpose the daily urban system is a good guide to what
exists now, although not necessarily to future requirements. For the
second and third purposes, the character and density of land uses and
the volume of social and economic interactions are important guides.
But for operational purposes, the nature of public powers and the kind of
planning systems which exist or could be created are critical factors.

The Goals of Urban Planning
We will postpone discussion of the concept of planning itself until later
in this chapter and will first look at the general rationale for some form of
overall planning of the urbanization process. The aim is not to give a
description of actual policies but rather to establish some benchmarks
whereby the aims and performance of various government bodies might
be evaluated. This exercise is also useful for assessing the value and
potential of any future type of planning system, such as that discussed
in the last chapter. Still, the subject is so broad that much simplification
is unavoidable.

There is a long-standing debate about the merits and defects of
government planning as compared with those of free market systems.
This debate became somewhat submerged during the 1950s and
1960s, when it seemed that a mixed type of economy was becoming
increasingly established and acceptable and when critics of planning
concentrated much more upon its organizational problems than upon its

general purposes. Today, however, in 1981, the issue is again very much alive with a fresh polarization of opinion between the right-wing proponents of market systems and (theoretically at least) of minimum government and the left-wing advocates of radical change in political systems.

It is not possible to give here a full review of the debate. But it should be remembered that much of the case for government planning has been (and still is) based upon demonstrations of the unsatisfactory consequences or defects of market systems and equally that much of the present disillusionment with "planning" reflects a new appreciation of the corresponding defects of political and bureaucratic action. The two types of defects stand opposed to each other, and any final verdict upon the desirability of planning systems must assess the balance being struck between the two systems (government and market) and the balance of gains or losses to the community generally that is likely to result.[7]

The aims of planning cannot be understood as *simply* a corrective exercise of market forces, for two reasons. First, the aims in question may be positive and not merely corrective—for example, they may seek to direct the course of urbanization or to plan the future use of natural resources instead of just removing some of the (alleged or actual) defects of free markets. Second, it would in any case be impossible for government to act simply as a neutral adjuster of market forces. Government action brings in politics, and politics creates its own direction and momentum. The activation of new public powers establishes new political and organizational interests, which is of course the very basis for criticisms of the defects or unintended effects of government interventions.

There is no authoritative list possible of the goals of planning. One can only inspect the general arguments put up by advocates of planning, and naturally these arguments vary. It does seem fair, however, to picture planning as being concerned (in principle) with a number of social values. For ease of exposition these values are here reduced to four: *efficiency, environmental improvement, equality,* and *community.*

Efficiency. It can be claimed that the market promotes efficiency in the sense of maximizing consumer satisfactions for any given distribution of incomes. For example, in an urban setting each household can make its own trade-off between competing values—better housing versus a longer journey to work, access to central facilities versus a leafy environment, proximity to relatives versus upward mobility—and so on. Each business firm can make the same calculation. Land and property markets are supposed to reflect the aggregation of such preferences.

Yet individual preferences can also be mutually frustrating. Homeowners escaping to the rural fringe find thousands following them who block their views and congest the roads. Organizations building motorways, airports, or factories according to their own functional criteria sometimes damage and sometimes benefit other interests and individuals. Quick obsolescence can occur: for example, a shopping center near a road junction may be quickly superseded by another center placed near a newer and larger highway. Both a cause and a consequence of these situations is that in quickly changing urban areas, free land markets are very responsive but highly unstable. Individual choice has to be exercised under conditions of considerable uncertainty and also of unforeseeable gains and losses of a personal and material kind. Hence, pressure grows for imparting some degree of stabilization and predictability to the urbanization process through systematic regulation of land uses and activities.

Another aspect of efficiency is the coordination of investments in urban infrastructure and the control of development so as to realize overall economies. Many investments can yield economies of scale if their rate of utilization can be foreseen with reasonable accuracy; conversely, development patterns have a considerable impact upon the costs and efficiency of public utilities and other services. For example, scattered and low-density development increases servicing costs, and heavy concentration of employment produces high costs of transportation. Of course, if individuals or firms are willing to pay the high indirect costs of certain locations, it may be quite reasonable to allow them that option (although unfortunately this policy is seldom consistently applied). But unless much indirect waste and inefficiency are to be accepted, individual options still need to be provided within an overall framework of planning and not outside it. Indeed, advocates of planning would claim that the range of options can thereby be widened.

It is perverse simply to equate efficiency with public service economies. In principle the goal requires a balancing out of costs to both private and public decision makers and the achievement of a general development framework which is more satisfactory to citizens (for a given investment outlay) than any alternative pattern. This aim is so broad and difficult that it can be approached only through a learning process. The planning of development has also to be continually checked and monitored against the possible range of individual opportunities and shared lifestyles. Efficiency divorced from consideration of ultimate social goals and satisfactions leads inevitably to a technocratic type of planning.

Environmental values are the traditional concern of urban planning. Planners have traditionally required the separation of "incompatible" land uses and have specified minimum standards for housing densities, office and factory construction, road access, open space, and so on. The rationale of such methods is that they both improve the physical environment and prevent the overloading (or underloading) of activities in relation to such facilities as the transportation network. Still, this anatomical approach has come under attack for its hygienic, impersonal character, its insensitivity to the "muddled variety" of urban life, and its neglect of very variable social and economic pressures. Much but not all of this criticism is justified, since minimum environmental standards have a genuine value. Planners have increasingly been concerned with the environmental impact of large projects and with more selective improvements such as traffic-free shopping centers and the adaptation of old districts to new purposes.

Another aspect of environmental values is the protection of cultural, historic, and recreational resources on the ground that their long-term social value is not expressed in the prices of their land and buildings. These assets comprise both minor "amenities," which seem valuable only to local residents, and large-scale regional facilities such as London's theaters or royal parks, whose protection has proved beneficial to an enormous clientele of both citizens and visitors (and incidentally to the tourist industry). The fact that fine buildings, townscapes, and landscapes are increasingly valued and visited strengthens the case for their protection against development pressures.

The much broader meaning of conservation refers to natural resources of air, water, land, and energy. The pollution and rapid consumption of these resources constitutes a distinctive modern problem which is especially critical in large urban areas. Public regulatory agencies have been established everywhere to control sources of pollution and to improve the quality of air and water. Still, the concern of urban planning is potentially wider and extends to the long-term planning of development so as to conserve resources of energy, land, water, and clean air. The extent to which these resources should be placed under direct public management and control has become a critical issue in all countries.

Equality. The case for public intervention in the urban system has always had (in principle) a strong relationship to the perception of severe environmental and social inequalities. In European countries particularly, but also in the United States, the case for redeveloping the blighted areas of cities and for improving the general environment of the "working masses" figured prominently in reconstruction goals after World War II. This notion of "urban betterment" helped to make and sustain the general case for planning. Subsequent experience with the limitations of primarily physical measures of redevelopment led to a wider goal encompassing other causes of social and economic deprivation.

The difficulty and contentiousness of the equality goal requires us to consider its rationale more fully. Many liberals would argue that if more equality is desirable, the best way to achieve it is through greater equality in the distribution of wealth, leaving individuals to choose for themselves a better environment and lifestyle. Such a policy (it will be said) is preferable to paternalistic government measures that aim to overcome urban blight and deprivation directly. If one accepts the argument, it still requires radical political action, which may in practice be much harder to achieve than more direct remedial measures. Yet the argument also overlooks the efficiency and environmental arguments for planning and the particular relevance these have for deprived areas.

From the opposite extreme comes the argument that efforts at urban betterment will be ineffective or self-defeating because of the cultural or behavioral characteristics of the deprived urban population. For example, E. C. Banfield claims the existence of a "lower-class culture" that is defined by the shortness of an individual's horizon. Individuals sharing this culture will not make any sustained effort to improve their lot, even if given opportunities to do so, if they must sacrifice immediate gratifications. This description would apply, as Banfield admits, to many people who are not in fact deprived. (Some people might even consider Banfield to be talking about a general behavioral tendency in modern Western societies.) Conversely, the description would *not* apply to many people who have moved since 1945 from blighted areas to a better environment, often (at least in Europe) with the help of substantial public projects and subsidies. Thus it is quite uncertain how many people Banfield's cap would fit in any particular area. In any event, theories of this kind also fail to consider specific causes of urban inequality.[8]

It would seem that for intrinsic reasons economic inequalities tend to compound themselves within an urban setting. In modern Western societies variations are much larger in respect to capital wealth than in respect to incomes, but it is capital that gives access to a better dwelling and an improved environment. Mortgage assistance spreads the opportunities of home ownership but still leaves wide differences in the homes that can be afforded. Public and cooperative housing schemes in many countries reduce the significance of capital inequalities but are least effective in aiding the poorest groups. These sometimes have the protection of rent controls, but the price is usually bad maintenance and property deterioration. The benefits and amenities of different urban locations seem often to vary more widely than comparative differences in income would warrant.

The processes of environmental differentiation tend to be cumulative. In the worst favored areas, physical blight, economic decline, and social deprivation are often combined. Irrespective of the question as to how far these processes cause or influence each other, one result is to reduce or eliminate the incentives upon private owners to make improvements unless others will do likewise and to transfer the whole burden to public authorities who may be unlikely or unable to respond adequately. Again the many "externalities" of development decisions are unevenly spread, partly for reasons connected with urban structure. Residents in old and congested urban areas suffer the most intensive blight from new road schemes or from air and noise pollution but are least likely—if only for reasons of cost and space—to benefit from a new public park. The relatively slow rate of changes in land use, compared with those in the economy, may reinforce the inequalities of the urban system.

In addition, technological change independently affects environmental opportunities. Thus users of private and of public transport have completely opposite interests with respect to the location of facilities and the use of streets and transportation modes. The former benefit from dispersed facilities which reduce traffic concentrations and ease access by car to individual sites, whereas the latter benefit from concentrated facilities and higher densities which assist access via public transport. If the former interest dominates, the latter will suffer, as will certain parts of the city—notably the inner areas and "corridor communities" through which traffic passes. These differential effects have a definite but partial relationship to income distribution, since the old and handicapped, children, many wives, and (at times) most people are dependent upon public transport whether or not they can afford a car. Suburbanites have acquired increasingly good road access to country parks, historic houses, beaches, and other facilities hundreds of miles away, while to travel a few miles within the inner city to a park or other facility has become more difficult, whether by bus or car. Here technological change has tended to reinforce, but also to shift, environmental inequalities.

There is also the important question of how far a favorable location secures differential advantages in the provision of public services such as education, health, police and fire protection, street cleaning and lighting, garbage collection and so on. Clearly it will do so if richer areas form separate local government areas which can then provide and charge for better services. But even if public services are nominally equalized across broad urban areas—the more usual situation in many European countries—the better locations will still benefit inasmuch as (1) more qualified public servants, for example, teachers, will usually prefer to work there; (2) their residents will usually be more articulate and influential over demanding services; and (3) there may be cultural bias on the part of professional officers and others toward the needs of different areas—although the reverse bias can occasionally apply. How far such influences actually operate depends upon social perceptions as well as the political balance of interests and upon the impartiality and efficiency of the public service. But even if there is considerable impartiality and uniformity in general, the residents of poor and blighted areas are still likely to suffer some degree of deprivation where public services are concerned.

Community. Planning is strongly and indeed increasingly concerned with what may be called community values. The ideological bias of planning is geared traditionally toward the discovery of community "objectives" which rest on some type of political consensus. Planning has to come to terms with the existence of social and political conflict, but too much conflict is dysfunctional because it prevents any real agreement on basic goals. This is one reason why planners often resist the politicization of planning and why an independent status is often sought, particularly in the United States, for planning agencies or commissions. The independent status is often illusory—for example, the traditional type of city planning commission in the United States rested in fact on the support of civic and business leaders interested in the pursuit of "good" or efficient government. Politicization of planning cannot in practice be resisted, and American planners in particular have increasingly seen themselves as technical auxiliaries to whoever holds political and executive authority. But unless the political system itself is capable of delivering a degree of consensus about goals, there will in a democracy be little continuity or consistency over the uses of planning.[9]

A basic issue is how community is to be conceived. There is a bias in planning thought toward stressing the rights of local communities to determine their own policies and future. This tendency is encouraged by the widespread reaction against "big government," and by the increasing stress in planning practice upon "public participation." It is local people and interests whose participation is often wanted or encouraged. Still, this stress upon local community claims is frequently inconsistent with the also espoused values of efficiency and equality. The local community is frequently highly conservative in the defense both of its social character and of its property and fiscal interests. Such local defensive action can (and frequently does) vitiate the goals of metropolitan planning for which a broader constituency (the metropolitan area or urban region as a whole) has to be postulated and if possible institutionalized in some form.

An important goal, often expressed although its meaning is vague, is that of the "well-balanced" community. At a minimum, it is said, local communities should not become too differentiated with respect to incomes, social class, ages, and stages in the life cycle of the individuals who compose them. This argument criticizes the market because it is *too* efficient in locating individuals according to their income and their social status or aspirations. What precise reasons are there for resisting such a trend?

Plenty of evidence suggests that most families and individuals prefer homogeneous to diversified neighborhoods, but there are still advantages in aiming at a "mixed society" within the broader confines of a town or a district in a large city. Access to schools and other social facilities, as well as the tax burden, would be spread more equitably. Equally important, some degree of proximity between social groups, at any rate within the umbrella of the same civic concerns, should have a therapeutic and educational effect over the reduction of social or racial tensions. Although this effect has not been clearly demonstrated, it seems likely in the long run. A related argument for a degree of social integration notes the "natural" complementarity of ages and lifestyles. The aged may prefer—or feel impelled by social custom—to live in Florida (if they can afford it), but old and young thereby lose satisfactions which they could gain from each other.[10] Ultimately the choices should be those of individuals—but market choices over location seem excessively geared toward the preferences of the "dominant consumer"—typically pictured as the male head of a household with a good income and two cars. The needs of less powerful consumers—such as old people, working wives, and perhaps teenagers—deserve more attention, which means that planning should influence development patterns and the location of facilities for the advantage of these other groups. These broader social goals often conflict with local interests.

We can now summarize some points about these various values or goals. First, each goal has both broader and narrower dimensions. For example, efficiency can be conceived in terms of the layout of a local district or an entire urban region; environmental values can seek to protect a local park or a broad "greenbelt." Second, each goal can be more narrowly or broadly interpreted—this point has just been made in relation to the "balanced" community. Third, these values are to some extent in conflict. This point applies particularly to the application of the equality and community criteria. Thus equality not only stands for some specific aims but is relevant to the pursuit of all other values, because every substantive policy has distributive implications. The efficiency goal, for example, would be vitiated in many people's minds if it widened inequalities, although it might simultaneously benefit a substantial majority.

Although the application of these values arouses conflicts, some of a basic kind, there are, as we have seen, some persuasive reasons for government planning. So far I have noted certain failures and limitations of market systems but have not considered the corresponding dysfunctions of government which may vitiate planning in practice. There are two such basic failings: technocracy and a political dysfunction.

Technocracy, or "bureaupathology," is a failure developing primarily within the administrative system. For example, just as land markets are excessively volatile, so planners may be excessively slow in bringing about the development or reuse of land, through overcommitment to an original plan. This failing is shown by the considerable number of vacant sites in British cities which still await their intended developer (often a public agency short of funds but sometimes a private developer who has not appeared) after twenty or more years. A worse failing still is the imposition of technocratic opinions or ambitions upon dependent clients of public agencies. Public housing policies, discussed in the next chapter, provide the clearest example of this trait. These dysfunctions are tendencies, not inevitable results, as can be seen from public projects which are quite free of them. Also they can be alleviated by methods of political control and public participation.

The greatest *political dysfunction* of planning is its tendency, despite proclaimed intentions to the contrary, to fail to reduce—or actually to increase—urban inequalities. There are two explanations of this result. One is the neo-Marxist explanation that public planning, far from controlling market forces, is itself subservient to the structural requirements of capitalism. Consequently it is bound to augment, not reduce, the inequalities associated with capitalism. These theories[11] are too elaborate and too formidable for review here. To some extent they run into contradictions—for example, an increase in public housing can be explained as a necessary support for the reproduction of the labor force required by capitalism, while a cut in public housing can be explained as an essential economy for protecting market profits.

Again, we might agree that government planning is circumscribed by the structural requirements of capitalism without also conceding that urban inequalities cannot be reduced in a capitalist society. Indeed, the very different policies followed and results achieved among such societies caution one against dogmatism. To the extent that these structural theories are correct, there would seem to be no remedy for urban deprivations except for a shift to the alternative inequalities of communist systems. In fact, even if there is a partial truth in some neo-Marxist analysis, the inequalities can often be explained adequately by others means.

The obvious explanation of continued inequalities is the skewed nature of political power. The richer, better organized, and more articulate interests are capable of reaping the major benefits of government interventions for themselves. This explanation is very simplified and also contingent. The actual impact of planning upon the equality goal will vary a good deal with the nature of political and organizational systems. This subject is taken up in the next section, where we will see that to some extent the political conditions necessary for effective planning are also congruent with the requirements of greater urban equality.

The Meaning and Conditions of Planning

No distinction has yet been drawn between the impact of public policies generally and planning as a specific kind of activity. Still, there are three criteria whereby the existence of planning might be identified, although they are all partial and questions of degree.

First, planning has an intellectual or analytic dimension which refers to the amount of thought and foresight put into the making of decisions, the number of factors considered and alternatives canvassed, and so on. Questions here concern not only the logical or technical tools that are employed but the extent to which societal problems can be tackled in terms of their intrinsic scale and complexity. For example, policy issues in fields like energy or transportation have become closely interlinked through technological and economic developments.

A second criterion is the extent to which government action aims to have a positive impact upon the course of events instead of merely responding to environmental changes supposed to be unforeseeable or uncontrollable. Under "trend planning" factors, such as the rate of economic growth, changes in consumers' demands or technological developments become exogenous determinants of public policies, and the actual or potential influence of governmental action upon them is tacitly or deliberately minimized. Planning, however, implies some positive efforts by governments to move in desired directions, even though the pace of execution may sometimes have to be modified or revised.

Third, planning implies some integrated and coordinated use of public powers. Once again, as with the other criteria, the achievement of this condition is always extremely partial. Planning systems do not remove political and organizational conflicts, but they can transform their nature by creating broader frameworks of public action. In favorable circumstances a planning system can impart a dynamic to public action which would otherwise be lacking and can reorder the continuing partisan conflict and accommodation between political and organizational interests.

Where all these conditions are met, some form of *comprehensive planning* can be said to have occurred. All planning implies some organizational framework, and there are several frameworks for comprehensive planning. One such is the coordinated exercise of powers by a multifunctional unit such as a city government in pursuit of general objectives. Another example is the planning done by a coordinating agency in some broad field such as transportation or energy policies. A third example is planning by a multipurpose public corporation or special agency. A fourth is a broad interorganizational agency such as a regional planning body. The planning actually done by any of these agencies may be so limited or ineffective as not to qualify.

A common error in discussions of comprehensive planning involves identifying this activity with a powerful central agency issuing instructions in a hierarchical or dictatorial manner. Although such agencies can of course exist, this is a quite unrealistic view of the planning which is possible or indeed desirable in Western democracies. Comprehensive planning is better viewed as providing a framework for the more limited plans prepared by functional agencies. The comprehensive planning agency will, it is true, need some effective powers, such as the authority to lay down guidelines for other agencies and to override them or act directly on occasion, but its effectiveness still turns upon mutual dialogue and harmonization of objectives.

Planning is an organic rather than a mechanistic process; it entails teamwork between individuals whose contributions should be judged according to their knowledge, not their status, and it works to some extent through the influence of ideas. Of course, planning will remain ineffective without access to political authority. One should not, however, underestimate the importance of new formulations of social problems and possible answers to them—of what Sir Geoffrey Vickers terms "appreciative" judgments—for the development of planning. For example, innovative thought of this kind is essential for the integration of professional techniques.[12]

Three criticisms are often made of the concept of comprehensive planning. The first is that it is *intellectually* difficult or impossible because a great number of factors must be considered and evaluated and because of the frequent ignorance of planners compared with the experts or managers of some functional agency.[13] This problem points again to the need for mutual dialogue. The intellectual limitations of the planning agency should also be balanced by its broader social and organizational perspective.

In the United States particularly, the concept of planning as a form of rational decision making is widely applauded and recommended for use by all public agencies (as well as by foreign governments seeking aid). The model used is often that of the big business corporation. When this prescription is enjoined upon a large and growing number of government agencies, which unlike business firms enjoy perpetual existence, it easily serves to rationalize narrow organizational viewpoints. Each agency may plan in a way which is procedurally rational but substantively irrational. Often the intellectual risks of more comprehensive planning seem less than those of organizational myopia.

Second, comprehensive planning is criticized for being (actually or potentially) tyrannical and inimical to liberty. Yet planning agencies have to cope with functional agencies which often have superior power and resources. Regional planning agencies, for example, usually find it hard indeed to exercise much influence over big public or private developers. The planning problem usually relates more to ineffectiveness than to tyranny.

There is a different sense, however, in which the criticism might hold. In a general way the pursuit of planning aims depends on the accumulation of sufficient public powers, so that a bias is created toward the growth of such powers. Moreover, when frustrated, a planning agency may seek additional powers in order to overcome some unforeseen factor which is blocking implementation of its plan. The desirability of any new power needs to be tested not only for its social utility but for its effects on liberty, and planning is not exempt from this requirement. Planning certainly *should* lead to some changes in the availability of public powers because of the redefinition of objectives, but planning can achieve much through redeploying and sometimes simplifying powers which already exist.

The third criticism is that in Western democracies comprehensive planning is impossible or utopian. This criticism, of course, is the opposite of that relating to tyranny and is far more plausible, particularly in respect to the United States. Some American writers try to save planning by ridiculing and rejecting any comprehensive approach, instead repackaging the concept as a sort of incrementalism—reaching some desirable goals in a piecemeal, adversary manner.[14] This "defense" of planning throws out the baby with the bathwater.

The scope for planning hinges upon political and organizational conditions. Modern democracies work through some mixture of representative leadership, pluralism, and populism. *Representative leadership* is built upon the ballot box and the mass political party. In principle it confers considerable discretion upon the elected leader or leaders of the executive branch to decide issues in the general interest. Party manifestos are usually too vague and transient to settle detailed policies, although they impart a general direction to government policies. Pressure groups can be to some extent kept at bay by virtue of the popular support and political legitimacy residing in the leadership, especially if the "majority choice" theory behind the system can be clearly seen to be working. The same circumstance at least enables and may require the leadership to take account of large latent interests (for example, the aged and the poor) who may be themselves weakly organized.

Pluralism implies a high level of organized group activity. Elected representatives and public agencies are both highly sensitive to group pressures, and policy decisions emerge from bargaining and accommodation between group interests. In theory pluralism enables most interests to be represented and social or ideological cleavages to be avoided through the overlap and diversity of individual interests. In practice pluralism is marked by very different degrees of influence which turn upon the size, wealth, cohesiveness, intensity of interest, leverage for joint action, and other qualities of the relevant or potential groups; it is also marked by the difficulties of holding the leaders of the interest groups accountable to their frequently passive membership.

Populism refers to the increasing pressures for democratic participation within either a political framework (for example, referenda) or an administrative one (for example, plan preparations, social and opinion surveys, and so forth to discover public wants). Populism has grown through dissatisfaction with both representative leadership and pluralism, but because of widespread public ignorance and apathy, populist techniques are open to manipulation by special interests and the media. Populism can, however, function as a guide to and support of executive leadership and a check on the claims of interest group leaders (for example, through opinion surveys), and "consumers' populism" is an important mechanism for making the provision of public services more responsive to the needs of clients.

All Western democracies, as noted previously, contain elements of majoritarianism, pluralism, and populism. The mixtures vary considerably, however. The United States displays a high degree of political and administrative pluralism, which stresses the brokerage rather than the leadership function of politicians, augments the influence of client groups and the degree of agency "autonomy," and impedes coordinated policymaking and planning. Still, elected chief executives—the president, state governors (to a much lesser extent), and the mayors of some cities—provide focal leadership for broad-based interests. In European democracies, the elected government possesses a much stronger legitimacy to act discretionally on behalf of majority or generalized interests, a legitimacy both reflected in (and derived from) a much more integrated administrative system. This situation strengthens the influence of career officials and professionals, and where the majoritarian basis of politics is in fact weak (as in the French Fourth Republic), it loads greater power on these officials. In all democracies, however, there has been a steady movement away from the majority-supported leadership concept and toward pluralism and, more recently, toward populism.

How do these features of political systems affect planning? The representative leadership principle can be much more favorable to planning than pluralism because the elected leaders have more scope to prepare and promote a coordinated use of public powers, provided they have a firm enough electoral base. Pluralism, by contrast, requires shifting and piecemeal accommodations between interest groups. Second, the discretion vested in political leaders enables them, if they so choose, to give professionals a positive and imaginative role over plan preparation, whereas with pluralism planners will function more as technical auxiliaries. The comparision is not as favorable to representative leadership as these points suggest, however. Where elected leaders come under the influence of special interests, there will be less counterweight from other interests than in a more pluralist system, and professional planners or other experts may be more able to pursue technocratic policies which flout the wishes of their final clients or other sections of the public.

Generally a stress on representative political leadership gives more weight to the interests of the underprivileged than does a more pluralist system. After 1945 this circumstance tilted public planning in countries such as Britain, Sweden, or the Netherlands toward relatively egalitarian and welfare-minded goals. Public powers were strengthened and local interests were to some extent overridden in the interests of broader majorities. Yet in retrospect it can be seen that some privileged groups were remarkably successful in using the planning system to their own advantage and in achieving increased profit opportunities in some areas so as to balance, or more than balance, those lost elsewhere.

The good postwar reputation of planning also owed something to popular perceptions of the success of governments in mobilizing wartime resources, at any rate among the victorious nations, and to the public's high expectations of economic and physical reconstruction, especially where cities had been bombed and devastated. The wartime ethos of solidarity carried over into postwar reconstruction and gave an egalitarian impetus to postwar plans. Experiences of food shortages and rationing also strengthened the case for land-use planning and for treating land as a vital common resource, a belief already well entrenched in the history of a small country such as the Netherlands, where land reclamation and development had for long been critical government functions.

Some broad-based interests were also supportive of planning. In Britain, for example, agricultural and rural interests wanted the protection of planning against indiscriminate development, and regional interests wanted industrial location controls and incentives to raise employment levels. In the towns planning profited from its connections with public housing and other measures (such as urban redevelopment and new towns) for the reduction of urban squalor and congestion. The direct advocacy of planning was in the hands of small, voluntary groups, but the policies of the main parties were influenced by the range of generalized interests favorable to a comprehensive planning program. Although the policy emphasis of the two main parties (Labour and Conservative) differed somewhat, both subscribed to a package of public measures which included regional development policies, agricultural and rural conservation, comprehensive redevelopment of blighted urban areas, new towns, and tough forms of development control. This degree of political consensus lasted to some extent into the 1970s, although on one important and in some ways vital issue—the treatment of land values—considerable and increasing party conflict occurred.[15] The political basis for some consensus of planning aims has gradually evaporated in Britain and other Western European countries for reasons which I will consider in the last chapter.

In the United States the New Deal period represents the closest parallel of a strong elected government responsive to the interests of a relatively poor majority (or, more accurately, an electoral coalition of underprivileged minorities). This period is still often viewed nostalgically as a golden age for public planning in the United States, not just because of its political bias, but because of President Roosevelt's experiments with new agencies (such as the National Resources Planning Board) which were reaching toward a more forward-looking and wide-ranging use of public powers. In retrospect this period appears politically unique, while "planning" under the New Deal was actually tentative and fragmentary. Nevertheless, the New Deal era does perhaps suggest that political conditions in the United States, as in other countries, could once again move in favor of a more positive use of public planning.

Powers and Organizations

Planning for an urban region depends on the public powers available and the kind of organizations which deploy them. It is worth listing some of the more relevant powers and some significant national differences in their availability and use.

Town Planning

The strength and purpose of land use regulation varies considerably. In the United States zoning is almost wholly under the control of local governments, with little review by state governments, although periodic constitutional decisions by the law courts have influenced its development. Zoning ordinances are laws passed by the local council, but variances can be granted by a board of appeal and ad hoc revisions ("spot zoning") made by the city council. There has also been increasing scope under these laws for planning agencies to deal flexibly with major or special applications. In practice zoning laws seem to be strongly correlated with the attempted maximization of property and land values. In small rich suburbs zoning may be very rigid indeed, thus maintaining high house prices and an exclusive character. Frequently, however, there is substantial "overzoning" of permitted industrial and commercial uses and of residential densities in less attractive areas. The old zoning code for New York City, the first such code to be produced, would have permitted a theoretically maximum population of 365 million persons in the city, and this code was replaced by a new and still very liberal code only after many attempted revisions. The rationale is to allow ample scope for development and for potential increases in land values except in expensive suburbs. For the same reason it is extremely difficult ever to prohibit development on open or agricultural land in private ownership, although in California there has been some success (through state action) in establishing protected coastal zones and a few zones of intensive horticulture.[16]

In Great Britain, and in most European countries, local plans are more flexible documents than American zoning laws. They also usually require central government approval, often after a public inquiry. Because of the general character of these plans, and long delays in their preparation and approval, there is in Britain considerable administrative discretion in the control of changes in land use. Local government has the power of "development control" to prevent such changes although it can be overruled by appeal to a central minister or an inspector acting on his behalf. A notable feature since passage of the 1947 Town and Country Planning Act is the right of local government to prohibit any *intensification* of land use (other than certain "tolerances" such as a 10 percent addition to capacity upon redevelopment) without incurring any liability for financial compensation. This sweeping power has afforded considerable protection to good agricultural land, greenbelts, and so forth and has enabled planners to concentrate new development in specified areas. Such power is much less effective in relation to the redevelopment of cities, where owners are entitled to substantial compensation if the intensity of land use is reduced.[17]

Turning to the "positive" powers of local governments to promote development, one finds some striking national similarities and differences. One almost universal example of this activity is the redevelopment of parts of city centers in order to achieve modern layouts and new, usually larger structures such as shopping centers, office blocks, and cultural centers. "Modernization" of this kind has typically been hindered by fragmented land ownership and obsolete road layouts. The bombing of many European cities in World War II created a direct imperative for redevelopment. Planning has proceeded either by public land assembly followed by sale/lease to private developers and public agencies (United Kingdom, France) or by schemes for pooling and reallocating parcels of land among existing owners (Germany). The rationale has been that only public initiative could achieve necessary results, but the actual results have depended not a little upon the interests of private developers and the extent to which they have been forced or persuaded to comply with broader community aims.

In addition, many other powers exist to redevelop blighted urban areas, but there are substantial national differences in their range and use. In Britain, under laws enacted in 1944 and 1947, local governments were given extensive powers to designate (after a public inquiry) "blitzed" and "blighted" areas for redevelopment, to acquire all the land, to demolish obsolete housing and "nonconforming" industries or other structures, and themselves to build new housing, social facilities, parks, shops, and factories or to lease land for these purposes. In the United States, by contrast, urban redevelopment under the Housing Act of 1949 aimed to attract private developers into blighted areas and so did little to remake the environment for the existing population, which was largely displaced.

Moving from the urban core to the urban frontier, one encounters equally striking differences in national practice. In the United States local governments play virtually no part in the promotion of new growth, apart from zoning and the provision of utilities. In Europe, however, they often have extensive powers to plan and to undertake new urban development. In Britain, local governments have much the same powers to buy land for public housing and other purposes that they have to redevelop blighted inner areas. In Sweden, local governments generally acquire in advance most of the land that will be needed for urban growth of all kinds and undertake much of the development themselves or supervise it closely.

In addition, central governments play some direct part in initiating new development. Under the 1946 New Towns Act a minister in the United Kingdom can designate an area for a new town and can appoint a development corporation with powers to acquire any of the land at pegged prices and to build or lease land for building houses, factories, offices, shops, and so on. In France, mixed development companies are created in accordance with centrally approved plans in order to acquire land and promote major new developments. This device is freely employed by groups of communes, and they and other public authorities own a majority of the shares in these companies. The nearest equivalent in the United States was the now discarded New Communities Act, which went no further than underwriting mortgage finance for any private or public developer starting an approved "new community."

Housing

Housing is the largest type of land use and the single most important factor in the quality of urban life. Moreover, in most countries housing and planning policies developed together as related forms of social betterment. The original stress upon slum removal widened out into broader measures for a complete upgrading of the whole residential and physical environment.

By the end of World War II, this conjunction of social beliefs was being propagated in all Western countries, but much more vigorously in Europe than in North America and particularly strongly in Britain with its old industrial legacy, strong labor movement, wartime bombing, which exposed new opportunities, and small but vigorous philanthropic movements for better housing and planning which had already spawned the garden city movement. In the United States similar social and philanthropic beliefs flickered during the New Deal period and influenced the 1949 federal Housing Act, but their impetus was very much weaker, given the generalized beliefs in private enterprise and self-help, the economic and political weight of land and development interests, a weak radical movement, and no wartime bombing. Most European countries were closer to the British position, and in Sweden welfare goals for housing and planning were vigorously entrenched. These traditions are important for their influence upon the approach of big cities to comprehensive planning in the post-1945 era.

Most European countries, unlike the United States, have developed very large public or nonprofit housing programs as a way of improving social welfare. Frequently these programs are entrusted to or controlled by local governments, thereby establishing an intimate functional and political connection between housing and planning. Public housing has therefore served both as the spearhead for many redevelopment projects (often on its own, since in blighted areas there has been little demand for private housing) and as a major determinant of new urban growth. Moreover, the conjunction of aims accounts for the powers conferred upon local governments in Britain or Sweden to accompany their housing developments with associated facilities providing industrial employment, shopping facilities, recreation, and the like for the residents. In recent years, it is true, the old links between housing and town planning have become somewhat attenuated, partly because of sharp reductions in public housing programs, and partly because planning has become more linked with transportation.

In the United Kingdom, almost half of total postwar housing between 1945 and 1975 was built by local authorities for rent (although Conservative governments have encouraged sales to tenants), and about one in three persons now lives in a "council house." In Sweden, a still higher proportion of housing was "nonprofit," built partly by local authorities and partly by cooperatives. In France, about two-thirds of all housing was provided by publicly controlled and financed bodies, including local government and "mixed societies." By contrast, in the United States public housing is statistically negligible, being only about 1.0 percent of the total housing stock, though of local importance in some big cities like Chicago and New York.

In the European countries the tenants of public or nonprofit housing are drawn from a wide range of income groups, although the poorest groups are underrepresented because of low mobility except where they are directly affected by slum clearance. Even so, type of housing tenure remains a significant indicator of perceived class differences in European countries. In the United States public housing is primarily for low-income individuals who have no other resource and consequently carries a stigma, partly too because there is so little of it. Thus local opposition to public housing projects in cities like Chicago is easy to understand, but such opposition can also be significant in British and European cities.[18]

In European countries, public finance for local housing programs is provided by loans and subsidies from central governments. The governments, therefore, influence the volume of such housing, specify standards, and influence or sometimes control rents. In France, as in some other countries, the Caisse des Dépôts et Consignations, a central agency, attracts small savings and provides loans for local housing and town planning projects. In the United States, such savings are channeled into private housing, and the savings and loan associations have been bitter opponents of public housing—a striking cultural and political difference from the French situation.

Government housing policies also everywhere include assistance to owner occupiers in the form of tax rebates, mortgage insurance or assistance, and other devices. Only in the United States is this policy completely dominant over direct public provision. There the postwar failure of the public housing program was followed in 1961 by the extension of federal mortgage insurance to low-income buyers and renters who had previously been shunned by the Federal Housing

Administration as bad risks. In Europe there is political conflict between right-wing and left-wing parties, with the former dedicated to owner occupation and often dubious or antagonistic toward public housing. As aid to owner occupiers in Europe has broadened, the tendency has grown for the large nonprofit housing sector to be reduced or sold off. Generally speaking, government aid to owner occupiers has no direct relation to urban planning, but has indirectly financed suburban expansion everywhere.

Employment

Public authorities are able to control the location of employment much less than that of housing. Local planning or zoning schemes restrict the sites which may be used for industry, offices, or commerce, and the densities thereon, but so many alternative sites usually exist that the volume or types of employment cannot be effectively allocated. Local governments can also attract industry by devices which variously include tax rebates (United States), publicity, the provision of infrastructure, or the building of flatted or other factories for rent or sale (United Kingdom). Such policies can support local plans, but especially in recessions there is so much total demand for available mobile industry that locations are primarily determined by the wishes of employers.

The most effective, but still limited, locational policies are those exercised by central governments; for example, in the United Kingdom, and Sweden, there is an elaborate structure of fixed incentives related to zone of location, with assistance for training, local utilities, and housing for key workers. In the United Kingdom industrial estates are built by government corporations, and there are also direct controls over the location or extension of large factories (over 5,000 square feet); in some regions for a time office developments were also controlled. In France there are similar policies, although in other European countries (Germany, Sweden), government uses incentives exclusively instead of controls.

Firms are now more mobile, and public infrastructure and service costs are high. As a result, there is an enhanced theoretical rationale for governments to guide or control the location of employment. At the localized level this theory prescribes detailed planning of sites so as to facilitate efficient operation, a good working environment, congruence with adjacent land uses, and good access for workers. Local planning powers for these purposes may be strong or weak and well or badly used but in any case cannot ensure the supply of employment in the desired places. For this purpose national inducements (or occasionally deterrents) may be used to guide firms *between* regions and regional or local inducements to determine sites *within* the region. Urban regional planning operates at the second of these levels and is sometimes supported, sometimes frustrated by national priorities between regions where such priorities exist.

Transportation

In all countries the provision of highways, public rail and road transport, ports, and airports is very largely—and sometimes almost completely—the responsibility of public agencies. Thus in contrast to employment or private housing, ownership in theory offers no obstacle to integrating transportation into a comprehensive urban plan. In practice many difficulties derive from the multiplicity of agencies and their dominance by quasicommercial and specialized policy criteria. A city which builds roads and owns the local transport system must still work within a hierarchy of highway authorities and control what is often a semiindependent public transport board having its own entrenched traditions and policies.

Massive highway developments have changed the face of most cities. Their destructive effects upon residential and urban environments, particularly but not exclusively in inner areas, and the related decline of public transport must be weighed against the increased mobility brought by increasing ownership of cars. Gradually a reshuffling of functions and journeys has occurred, with many more and longer crosstown journeys made by car and fewer total journeys to the center. City centers have become more specialized, and while the centers of the "world cities" have held their own or grown, many second-rank cities have been adversely affected.

These trends have been universal but have proceeded much faster in American than in European cities. Reasons include the larger and faster growth of car ownership in America, the quicker erosion there of public transport, and the greater cultural concern in Europe with traditional structure of cities. Belief in urban motorways reached its peak in Europe in the 1960s and has since declined. Subsequently there has everywhere been increased government subsidies for public transport, often achieved by reducing the funds available for highways. In the United Kingdom the 1967 Transport Act required local authorities to prepare programs for both roads and public transport for which consolidated grants were paid. In the United States the federal government has introduced aid for mass transit, but highways still receive the lion's share of support. The achievement of a better "modal split" between public and private transport users, and restraints on car usage in central areas by parking controls and other devices, has become a new orthodoxy.

Within urban regions the powers just discussed are distributed among a variety of public organizations. Occasionally the jurisdiction of a major government conforms fairly closely to the concept of the urban region. On a world scale the national governments of Hong Kong and Singapore, and in Germany the *Land* governments of Hamburg and Bremen, are effectively city regions. In Australia the heavy concentration of population in the state capitals, combined with the weakness of local governments, means that some state governments are primarily concerned with a capital region, which they effectively dominate. This is especially true of South Australia (Adelaide) and Western Australia (Perth). These situations have arisen almost by happenstance, however.

More usually an urban region constitutes an organizational and political crossroads or no-man's-land. Urbanization has transcended the frontiers of city governments and has become the concern of numerous local units of varying size and status. Metro governments have added a new dimension to the local government scene. Central and state governments increasingly intervene in urban affairs, although the actions of their departments are often weakly coordinated. A multitude of public corporations or joint local authorities also exists, often following independent lines of action. Regional planning agencies concerned with overall planning are often present as well, although they are frequently weak.

These organizations can be classified in ways which help to explain their behavior. A local government is partly defined as a body responsive to local interests and control and partly as a collection of services guided by different professional, technical, or welfare criteria. Generally the smaller the local government, the more locally responsible or accountable it will be—which is why local citizens often resist annexation. In the United States it is sometimes claimed that the values of this local control are more important (for the locals) than those of service efficiency or overall planning.[19] Big city governments are much less accountable in this sense and are more dominated by professional bureaucracies.[20] Still, city governments can also sometimes act as strong protagonists for the latent interests of underprivileged groups needing housing, jobs, and a better environment.

Public corporations are appointed usually by central or state governments but sometimes by cities or metros. Other special agencies are responsible to groups of local governments or are jointly appointed by central and local governments. These agencies are frequently concerned with transportation or public utilities such as water supply, sewerage, and so forth. Their behavior tends to be dominated by technical and quasi-market criteria. Although they often do not market services directly, they typically conceive their task in terms of meeting the potential demands of their consumers. If their financial status permits, they may overprovide the service or charge below cost in order to forestall criticism. They try to steer clear of political issues and to locate their activities (to the extent that doing so is technically possible) in such a way as to minimize opposition, they are often suspicious of overall planning, and they are also usually weakly controlled by their appointing governments. To the world they present a bland managerial face and are often only weakly distinguishable from business firms holding utility franchises.

Another distinctive type of body is the welfare agency concerned with housing, health, or welfare. These bodies are generally embedded, especially in European countries, within the structure of local government. In the United States, however, local agencies for such purposes as public housing and community development are frequently separately constituted and may possess considerable independence from the city government even when appointed by the mayor. Welfare agencies generally have a dependent and weakly organized clientele and are guided by professional criteria or sometimes by social idealism.

Besides local governments and regional planning agencies, a number of more specialized bodies may be assigned or may develop a stake in comprehensive planning in various ways. Some public corporations develop a variety of activities. For example, the Port Authority of New York and New Jersey, established by compact between the two states and appointed by their governors, developed an enormous public works empire of bridges, tunnels, highways, airports, bus terminals, and specialized buildings like the World Trade Center, besides its original port activities. The authority followed business criteria, charging for its facilities but using public powers to build them, and it took over tasks from local government because of its superior finances and business rating. Yet it neglected social goals—for example, it was reluctant to invest in commuter railroads. This example (and there are others) represents a form of technocratic planning, or perhaps one should say enterprise.[21]

Other types of development agencies are welfare-oriented. Many city governments in Europe pursued housing and planning goals jointly on a broad front. In South Australia the Housing Trust (appointed by the state government) gained powers to build industrial estates, develop town centers, and build a satellite town (Elizabeth).[22] In New York state the Urban Development Corporation was originally empowered to change local zoning, acquire land, and undertake town development both on virgin sites and on derelict land in the city, although its powers over zoning were later removed because of local opposition.[23]

The fullest examples of town-building agencies are the new town development corporations in Britain. These bodies to a large extent remove the planning of the town from the control of local government, subject to the supervision of the minister. This is a rare power; in France and elsewhere local governments are intimately involved in new town building. The power was withdrawn from the New York Urban Development Corporation, and its use would probably not be acceptable any longer in the United Kingdom, although more than thirty new towns have already been designated and developed in this way. The justification for this strong power is that the new town primarily serves the latent interests of a large incoming population, not the overt interests of the usually much smaller numbers already residing there. The new town corporations are examples of comprehensive planning within specific, limited areas. Their objectives are partly social (the provision of good housing, social facilities, and an attractive environment for the incoming population) and partly economic (the promotion of industry and commerce, the creation of an efficient pattern, and so on.) The increase in value of the publicly owned freeholds can be viewed as means to these ends rather than an end in itself. The range and coordination of their powers and the breadth of their goals mark these bodies clearly as comprehensive planning agencies, but their existence has usually stemmed from a broader regional framework of planning (see chapter 4).

Using the description of different types of organization and the concepts of overt and latent interests, we can gain some insight into the typical organizational conflicts which arise within an urban region.

1. There is competition between local government units over tax resources, government grants, and the location of facilities. Where planning and zoning powers are highly localized, as in the United States, these powers can be vigorously used on behalf of local interests. The nature of the result depends on the distribution of local power between residents of various kinds (for example, house and apartment dwellers), developers, and landowners. The result may be a "closed shop" or an "open door" or something in between; it will be the first if residents are rich and homogeneous enough to agree on defending the present character of their area and the second if land and development interests dominate. One result is foreclosure of suitable areas for people seeking homes. Conversely, where development interests dominate, overzoning in the pursuit of higher land values can cause wasteful and shoddy development patterns. The system stresses the value of local community control, but other values (efficiency, equity) are shouldered aside. For example, the benefits of land use stabilization and environmental protection, discussed earlier, are distributed very unequally.

In European countries local government units are usually larger and more uniform, and where they are not (for example, in France), they are under stronger central supervision. Local planning also takes place within a framework of broader county and/or regional plans. Professional planning influence is stronger, and local political power is weaker. Consequently there is more attention to such latent interests as economy in public service provision and protection of the best agricultural land. Conflicts over taxable resources are less sharp. Nonetheless the same conflicts occur on a broader scale and in a modified manner.

2. There are conflicts between local interests and developers of all kinds. Developers, who are often public authorities, mediate the latent interests of diverse publics for the supply of housing, water, and many other services. Local interests often have strong views regarding the location of these facilities—for example, easy access to a motorway may be valued, but not if it is driven through the local community. Because of the political interest developers have in minimizing opposition, the strongest local communities often succeed in these tussles at the expense of the weaker ones. Local opposition may be too strong everywhere to admit some facilities (a major airport or a nuclear power station), leading to further concentration of these activities on existing sites where the local opposition has already to some extent been defeated, although both efficiency and equity may be badly served thereby. Airport planning for London, New York, and other major cities exemplifies this tendency.

3. Also familiar is conflict between a city and its suburbs or exurbs, which can take several forms. One is competition for financial support from higher levels of government. In the United States lobbies seek funds in the state capitols and in Washington, whereas in Britain local authority associations maneuver more formally. Since 1974 the Association of Metropolitan Authorities, representing local government in the largest urban areas, has pressed its claims in competition with the County Councils Association. In Sweden and some other countries all local governments belong to the same association, which seeks to unify their claims. Not all suburbs are rich by any means, and the largest differences in wealth occur between suburban units. The biggest financial problems arise where the local economy is declining (as in many cities today) or population is growing very fast (as in many suburbs).

Cities often need to extend boundaries or to look beyond them in order to secure water, to find sites for houses, or for other purposes. If, as happens in Europe, cities have substantial extraterritorial powers, they take on a regional role and engage in conflicts with other local governments. A city building housing beyond its borders is acting directly to articulate the latent interests of its poorly housed citizens. Interests will diverge in other areas of regional planning. For example, cities often have a greater interest in good public transport and suffer more environmental damage from highway building. Other conflicts will arise between the "city users" (commuters to the center for work, shopping, and recreation) and the "city livers" (especially those living in blighted or declining areas). These conflicts will be expressed within the city government itself as well as between city and suburban units.

The next three chapters consider planning executed or attempted by three types of organizations. First come the efforts of central cities to use their concentration of powers so as to control their growth or combat their decline. Secondly are the efforts of metro governments to fulfill the overall planning role for which they were in part created. Finally come the regional planning frameworks created by central governments, often in partnership with local governments, in order to tackle still broader urban issues and to promote national urban policies where such exist.

2: Expanding and Declining Cities

Central Cities within the Urban Region

Before considering the plans and policies of the governments of big cities, I will review their physical location within an urban region and some of their organizational and political characteristics.

Local government is often highly fragmented within an urban region. A typical pattern shows a substantial central city surrounded by a large number of suburban and exurban local governments supplemented by an upper tier of local government in the form of one or more counties, departments, or other units, and often by a considerable number of special districts and other ad hoc authorities. There are significant national variations; for example, cities have traditionally been more important than counties in the United States or in Sweden, while in Britain until 1974 county councils were highly important in suburban areas but had no jurisdiction in central cities (termed "county boroughs"). Still, the actual degree of fragmentation varies very considerably, being greatest in the United States. A book was written about the 1,400 governments of the New York region[1] and the Chicago SMSA (not untypical) contains 6 counties, 120 municipalities, 29 townships, 154 school districts, and 196 special districts. By contrast, and at the other extreme, the average English provincial conurbation (which of course excludes London) contains now only 7 local governments and some special districts. Other countries fall in between, but often, as in France, there is a very large number of local communes or similar units. Local government has lately been considerably affected by "metro schemes," which are the concern of the next chapter.

Here the focus is on what is usually termed the central city. The central city occupies the traditional heartland of the urban region, but its size and structure are weakly related to geographic patterns. In a typical urban region, a substantial city center is surrounded by a dense urban core, often developed originally before 1914, and then by successive rings of more modern suburbs and exurbs, or there are sometimes several principal centers and urban cores. The governmental unit—the central city—is in some cases actually smaller than the urban core, however, while in others it is very much larger, embracing a considerable slice of suburbia and sometimes open country beyond. Generally the populations of central cities are declining steadily as a proportion of the total population of the urban region because of outward migration and the rigidity of their boundaries.

Explanations for the very variable but frequently restricted size of the central city are chiefly political and historical. Thus for British cities and for American cities in the East and Midwest the great era of city annexation or expansion came before World War I, when suburban obstacles to growth were fewer than subsequently. Cities showed very variable degrees of foresight during this period. Later, special advantages enabled some cities to expand; for example, between 1918 and 1939 Los Angeles used its monopoly of water supply to persuade some suburbs to accept incorporation.[2] Some cities have natural "green lungs" which they acquired without difficulty—for example, the large area of moorland within Sheffield (England). Again, in some federations particularly, cities may be kept small through the jealous control of a state government; thus the city of Sydney with 170,000 people contains only about 6 percent of the population of its metropolitan area, which is Australia's largest.

How is planning by these central cities affected by organizational and political influences? Let us first consider the tricky concept of "organizational interest." Any organization can be considered as dedicated to its own stability and growth. This means that it must in the first place procure the necessary inputs (money, staff, and legal authority) to perform its functions effectively. It will further be interested in maintaining an environment that is stable and hospitable toward its organizational goals and in expanding its activities where possible. Of course, these organizational "laws" or tendencies are subject to external tests of performance. A business firm is checked and guided by market tests and a public authority largely by political tests. The demands of clients for better or more public services will fuel expansion, but demands from taxpayers for economy will restrain growth and sometimes through political action will enforce retrenchment whatever the intrinsic tendencies of the organization. Thus it would be wrong to posit any absolute laws of organizational stability or growth; rather, we see a set of tendencies circumscribed by external criteria.

A further major limitation of such theories is that a public organization such as a city government is very much an "open system"—open, that is, to influences or directives from other public or sometimes private organizations. As suggested earlier it is part of a complex inter-governmental network. Its functions are not autonomously determined for the most part but are statutorily fixed and circumscribed. Many of its staff will consider that they belong to bureaucratic or professional cadres which have wider loyalties than to the city itself. Its politicians may belong to national political parties whose goals are indifferent to local interests. This interorganizational framework will also influence local perceptions of the interests of the city government. There will, for example, be a bias toward developing those functions which encounter least opposition from other public organizations.

"Organizational interest" therefore has limited explanatory power. For example, quite apart from the ambitions of mayors or officials, city governments often have an obvious organizational interest in expanding their boundaries in order to perform many functions, such as transporta-tion or housing, effectively. Unfortunately for them, such growth is often impossible.

To some writers the most obvious example or organizational interest is the need to protect or if possible enhance the local tax base. Paul Peterson argues that cities are forced to compete for mobile enterprises and/or wealthy citizens. For the same reason they cannot pursue redis-tributive policies which favor their poorer citizens because this will increase local taxation and drive out wealth. Peterson's analysis does show that in the United States redistributive policies are pursued in varying degrees by federal and state governments but very little by local governments, although there are difficulties over which services should be described as "redistributive" and to what extent. He concludes that, whatever its political coloration or ambition, there are very strict limits upon the pursuit of welfare goals by any city government, and that economic prosperity is in fact a dominant goal for every city.[3]

Peterson's theories are persuasive much more in relation to the United States than to other countries. It is true that national taxation is every-where both more progressive and more elastic than local taxation, so that welfare policies have largely to be funded at the national level, but such policies can be established or applied at the local level with the aid of national subsidies. While local government has again everywhere become much more dependent upon central government grants, the contribution of such grants to total tax revenues of local governments varies from about 35 percent in Sweden to 40 percent in the United States (including aid from states), 60 percent in the United Kingdom, and more than 90 percent in the Netherlands. Equally or more important is the extent to which such central aid is deliberately steered to localities with the weakest resources or greatest needs. Such equalizing effects, although everywhere complex and imperfect, show up weakly in the United States compared with most European countries.

The elasticity and acceptability of local taxation also varies considerably. In Scandinavian countries local income taxes provide a much more buoyant revenue source than do property taxes, which elsewhere are the staple and sometimes (as in the United Kingdom) almost the sole independent resource of local government. Local trading activities in some countries (for example, Sweden, Germany) yield a useful surplus, and in Germany there are substantial local taxes upon trade and industry. Everywhere there is a search for new sources of local revenue, although the quest is difficult.[4]

Thus the effects of local finance upon organizational aims vary very greatly indeed. In the United States it is a basic aim (Peterson would say necessity) of city planning to raise the property values which constitute the local tax base. In theory this aim might be pursued by municipal enterprise, for example, through the public ownership and leasing of land, but in practice political support for the market system bends the cities' efforts toward attracting business enterprises and raising land values generally. In European cities there is some (but much less) pressure to follow these goals. The greater financial dependence upon central government which often (but not always) results is also associated with greater policy dependence, even through the relationship between these factors may be indirect, as is the case in the United Kingdom. City governments are then relieved of some of the organizational pressures of resource competition at the cost of accepting policy directives from above. In favorable circumstances, however, the exchange may still leave the cities with considerable initiative to pursue their own goals within the framework of national inducements and controls.

The scope for initiatives by city governments seems everywhere to be declining, however. In the past many European cities regarded the state of the local economy as being largely beyond their control and concerned themselves more with cultural aims or welfare than with economic goals. Some fortunate cities have not had to bother much about their prosperity, at least not until recently. In England some city councils (such as that of Birmingham) have been dominated by businessmen and have been keen on commercial growth, while in others business may be weakly represented and uninfluential—as used to be true of London. Increasingly, however, city governments have become more politically concerned with local prosperity and employment, whether or not this concern is essential for protecting their tax base, as a consequence of a general decline in the economies of inner cities. Still, the cities' capacity to act has not increased, and their financial and policy dependence upon the center has grown. In different ways, depending upon the system, cities are caught between the goads of poverty and central dominance.

We next should consider the implications of political behavior for urban planning. There has been a long dispute in the political science literature as to whether policymaking in American cities is pluralist or elitist in character. Both propositions may be true of different cities. In any case the prospects for planning depend on the kind of pluralism or elitism. Several writers have commented on the tendency of city councils to avoid conflict and the consequent ability of interest groups to veto decisions. Thus even a strong mayor may be unable to mobilize political support for more positive planning. In Chicago politics, as described by E. C. Banfield, the mayor has enough reserves of power to arbitrate policy conflicts, but this is brokerage, not planning.[5] J. L. Pressman notes that in Berkeley the city government is directly responsible for only a small slice of local expenditure, the rest being handled by numerous special agencies. The council was unwilling to let the mayor take over functions such as the employment program when the opportunity arose or to give directions to the housing and redevelopment agencies, which he appoints.[6]

It follows that effective planning, in terms of any impact upon the city, is much more likely to be the work of an "independent" agency than of the city planning commission. Such action still requires strong political support, but generally this is of an elitist kind. In New Haven Mayor Lee lined up effective support for an ambitious program of urban redevelopment, and mayors achieved similar results in Atlanta, Boston, Newark, and many other cities. These programs depended upon the support of business interests plus the "organizational interest" of the city government in utilizing generous federal subsidies, and they were carried out by "independent" agencies which negotiated the use of the cleared sites and the federal financing. It proved much harder to harness such planning to welfare aims. In Newark, urban redevelopment was handed to the Public Housing Authority, which attempted to integrate the two programs (as the 1949 federal legislation envisaged) and to concentrate action upon the most blighted areas; but it increasingly found that it had to choose those sites and projects which interested private developers. The Chicago public housing plan represented another effort at comprehensive planning for welfare goals, but it was defeated by the opposition of the local aldermen on the city council to the proposed housing sites—a good example of the triumph of overt over latent interests and also of conflict avoidance by a city council.[7]

On the other hand elitism of a kind may be much more favorable to planning in some European countries, where the elite consists of elected councillors and professional officials who have a broad view of the desirable scope of city government and who are proud or ambitious about the city's achievements. The erstwhile London County Council (LCC) was outstanding among British and indeed world cities for the quality of its education and welfare services, for the scale, range, and variety of its public housing projects, and for its ambitious concepts of urban planning. Much the same could be said of the Stockholm City Council, and both these local authorities will receive further attention. Elitism exists in such cases in the sense that once elected, the councillors enjoy considerable freedom of action, and they in turn put considerable trust in paid officials of high professional caliber and standards. Stephen Elkin has argued that the London County Council was "depoliticized" compared with an American city, because pressure group activity was low and the citizens were complaisant, or anyhow uncomplaining.[8] Thomas Anton makes precisely the same points about the Stockholm leadership.[9] (Neither description would be so true today.) This sort of "representative elitism," as the system might be called, rests upon the support of disciplined political parties in local government. By contrast, party politics are weaker and more localized or are absent altogether in most North American cities.

Still, party politics in local government also have deleterious effects upon community involvement in planning issues. In the United Kingdom local elections are fought largely around national issues, and local issues of transportation, housing, and so forth are consequently downgraded. The low visibility of the local leadership weakens the political standing of cities in a national context. The more pragmatic and personalized politics of American cities avoid this situation, and their mayors provide more visible leadership and constitute a powerful lobby in Washington.

Both political and administrative conditions affect the status and influence of the agency responsible for city planning. In British and some other European cities, town planning is performed by a normal department which also controls development and discharges some other executive responsibilities—for example, urban redevelopment. The planning department's effectiveness depends upon close cooperation with related departments such as housing and transportation and upon the support of political leadership. As in the United States, the plans of these functional agencies can often have more impact upon the city than do the aims of the planners, but coordination is closer and more direct. In Britain in recent years the central coordinating machinery of many city governments has been strengthened, leading often to the development of a new form of "corporate planning" lodged in the chief executive's office and reporting to a policy and resources committee of the council. The relationship between the town planning and corporate planning functions is often difficult and uncertain. Still, there is more potential now for administrative integration if the nature of the planning function can be clarified.

In the United States, by contrast, the scope of the planning function has always been broad, but the function has traditionally been lodged in an "independent" city planning commission. The commission can prepare a "master plan" and proposals for land use zoning, but the zoning law itself (and its amendments) are the political prerogative of the city council, and appeals against zoning go to an independent board. The commission often prepares a capital budget also for the council's approval, but it has no leverage for coordinating departmental decisions and wields little or no executive power. The weakness of this machinery led Robert Walker and others to propose a long while ago that the planning function should be lodged in the office of the mayor or city manager and should be widened to include all the functions of the city government—a concept akin to that of corporate planning. In many cities this transfer of the planning function has now in fact occurred, although often its scope has not been widened or has even been reduced.

The planning function in American cities has never been satisfactorily located. The old system (which still continues in many places) gave the planners a certain detachment from immediate political pressures and permitted them to take a long-term view, but the influence of the planning commission depended usually on the support of civic and business leaders interested in "good government." The commission could often plan to any effect at all only by winning the support of key business interests, as described in Altshuler's studies of the Twin Cities.[10] Even where the commission had special powers conferred by a city charter, as in New York City, its effectiveness was very limited.[11] Removal to the mayor's or manager's office certainly gives the planning agency a more central political and administrative status but may also reduce external support for its activities. On balance, with many variations between cities, the planning agency's political effectiveness will be somewhat increased, but the planners' time horizons and broader ambitions may have to shrink.[12]

These organizational issues will be further discussed in the final chapter. In the account which follows, I emphasize the outputs of city planning, not its internal politics and machinery, but understanding of these internal features is necessary for an understanding of what cities do.

Expanding Cities and Regional Problems

After 1945 many European cities embarked upon ambitious schemes of redevelopment and expansion. This was an era of big city development machines backed by highly professional staffs and ambitious political leaders. Comprehensive planning was attempted with varying degrees of success. Cities were drawn into broader regional issues by their need for new outlets for urban development. In the process they collided with surrounding local governments, and their progress depended increasingly upon the support or arbitration of central governments. In this section the examples of British cities and Stockholm, the Swedish capital, will be used to explore the nature of the process and its results.

The cities in question were inspired by ambitious welfare goals. Central to these goals was the improvement of housing conditions by direct public action, and the link between housing and planning policies was strongest during this period. The final aim was to provide a satisfactory and separate dwelling for all eligible households that wanted one. This aim involved cities in accepting responsibility for large numbers of people living in bad or overcrowded housing, and the extent of crowding meant that slums generally had to be replaced by a much increased volume of new dwellings. But in addition cities accepted responsibility for a large proportion of the new households which were continuously being formed. Since standards of eligibility were fairly elastic and household sizes fell rapidly, the long housing lists of cities diminished little and even grew despite intensive building efforts. Stockholm's list of applicants grew from 23,000 in 1948 to 111,000 in 1970, partly because the city had lowered its standards of eligibility. It seemed almost as if cities wanted to accept larger housing burdens so as to fuel their own expansion.[13]

The target of better housing was closely related to broader planning aims. British cities such as Glasgow, Manchester, Liverpool, and Birmingham aimed to work their way right around the ring of decayed urban development which surrounded each city center by means of successive "comprehensive redevelopment areas." The city could thereby acquire all land within these areas and could demolish and rebuild extensively. The aim in each case was wholesale demolition of obsolete or badly sited buildings and the introduction of more rational layouts and modern buildings; for example, many old factories disappeared, although sometimes, as in Birmingham, new flatted factories were provided by municipal enterprise. There were also attempts notably by the London County Council, to plan for employment and social facilities on the large new housing estates. But of the cities in question, only Stockholm planned new development with a high degree of effectiveness.

The cities faced severe problems of space. Comprehensive redevelopment always substantially reduced the local population, because overcrowding was eliminated, new roads provided, and new standards applied to space around buildings and to schools, playing fields, and so forth. Initially, British planners kept the new housing densities fairly low (at least by European standards), although the Town and Country Planning Association, Lewis Mumford, and others were critical of the small provision made for single-family dwellings with gardens within these inner areas. Subsequently housing densities were raised to reduce the volume of population displacement. Even so, about a third to a half of the original population was generally displaced and added to the pressures for further public developments on the urban fringe. The process of redevelopment required cities to run fast in order to move a short distance toward their ultimate goal. Birmingham, for example, during the 1960s built 47,000 dwellings but demolished 35,000 for a net gain of only 25 percent of production. About one-third of these new dwellings were in the inner core of redevelopment areas, where the city had virtually a monopoly of new construction, and about two-thirds on peripheral estates. By 1971 38 percent of the dwellings in the city were publicly owned, 42 percent were owner occupied, and only 20 percent privately rented. The private rented sector had been displaced to a second ring of old and dilapidated housing which was increasingly filled with the city's postwar influx of colored immigrants.[14]

Cities therefore badly needed more land for development, which brought them into conflict with surrounding county and district councils. The counties exercised planning powers under the 1947 Town and Country Planning Act, and their financial and political interests were frequently opposed to those of the big cities. In this postwar period big cities tended to be Labour controlled, but the surrounding counties were predominantly Conservative. Thus there were lines of both organizational and political conflict, although counties were generally large enough to take a broader view of urban issues than smaller local units could. Cities had powers to develop beyond their boundaries, but disputes on this issue depended on the arbitration of central government under the terms of the 1947 act.

Central government policies in Britain (further discussed in chapter 4) favored the containment of the largest cities by means of greenbelts, wherein any substantial development would be prohibited, coupled with the creation of "self-contained" new towns and the expansion of existing towns at some distance from the cities. These policies were particularly applied to London but were influential elsewhere. The New Towns Act (1946) enabled eight new towns to be launched within the London region. Simultaneously a metropolitan greenbelt about five miles deep was established by joint action of the counties around London, and in 1951 the relevant minister refused the request of the London County Council to build yet another "quasi-satellite" on the capital's fringe. More slowly provisional greenbelts were established around other big cities, and some provincial new towns were started—two within the ambit of the Birmingham conurbation, three in Lancashire, four in the Scottish industrial belt. The Conservatives who were in power for thirteen years from 1951 continued after some hesitation with the development of existing new towns but for many years would create no more. They were influenced not only by prevailing ideas about urban planning but by the consideration that new towns helped the counties to resist urban expansion. It was a Conservative minister who in 1955 urged a wider application of greenbelts.[15]

The cities' view was that the new town program was too small and wrongly designed to help their housing problems very greatly. The new town development corporations urged, and the government agreed, that their growth should proceed by attracting industrial and other firms from the big cities and offering housing to the firms' workers. In most new towns the method worked and ensured a sound economic base and a balance of housing and employment. For the cities, however, the relief offered was indirect—"filtering,"—since most of the workers moving to new towns were in prosperous industries and frequently were not on the cities' housing lists. The cities' view was statistically correct, especially in relation to inner city areas.

To help meet this problem without more urban expansion, the government passed in 1952 the Town Development Act, which enabled a big city to export population and industry to distant sites in cooperation with the local district and county councils. The idea was not only to help big cities—as the minister put it, "If cities are not allowed to swell they must be enabled to hop"—but also to help restore the fortunes of stagnant or one-industry towns which might welcome growth. Though greased with some government aid, the implementation of the act made it necessary to overcome many hurdles: the distances involved, the complexity of the operation, and the need for cooperation among three local governments with quite different organizational and political interests. In these circumstances it is surprising that the act yielded as many as sixty operational schemes of town development, mostly too small to make much difference to big city problems although important to the participating localities.

In response to these policy changes, the London County Council took an increasingly broad view of its extraterritorial interests. Before the war it had built large housing estates beyond its borders. After 1945 it quickly built ten satellite communities on the capital's fringe, some large enough to hold 40,000 people. When disallowed by the minister from building a further satellite in 1951, the LCC had no option left but to use the Town Development Act, which its leaders attempted enthusiastically to do. Of more than one hundred projects discussed between local authorities, those in the richer rural and exurbanite areas generally failed, but joint projects with small industrial or railway towns were more successful. The LCC also attempted to build its own new town to an original design at Hook in Conservative Hampshire, which defeated the project but agreed by way of compensation to cooperate in two substantial town development schemes.

The LCC's search and actual projects were widely scattered, often well beyond the London region. One might wonder what conception of "organizational interest" led the LCC to finance housing and industry at Bodmin, 300 miles away, or to negotiate for the same purpose with Perth (Western Australia) halfway round the world. London was of course then a prosperous city, and the LCC was landlocked into a small area of declining population. Its leaders and officials were mostly convinced that some of their clientele would benefit from small-town life rather than the increasingly high-rise type of development within the capital, which was seen as the only alternative and one seemingly more costly, even after the costs of new infrastructure and industrial relocation had been taken into account.

Other big cities were involved more directly in greenbelt politics rather than the politics of far-flung dispersal. Birmingham fought the surrounding counties for the right of peripheral development, and Manchester tussled hard with Cheshire for the right to build one or two satellite towns inside that county. The government arbitrated these disputes through the medium of a series of hard-fought public inquiries which left Birmingham half-successful at best and Manchester defeated. The surrounding counties offered the limited alternative of small town development schemes, an inadequate and inferior arrangement for the cities (although they participated). Eventually the government designated several new towns in each region as a way of structuring growth and as a contribution to solving local conflicts. In Scotland the great city of Glasgow, plagued with problems of unemployment, squalor, and overcrowding, attempted to solve its problems through massive redevelopment at very high densities, nearly bankrupting itself in the process. The Scottish Office, however, followed a strong new town policy in the Clyde region and did persuade Glasgow to participate in some small town development projects in the remote Highlands and elsewhere.[16]

This history shows British cities struggling to maintain simultaneous policies of urban redevelopment and growth in the face of many obstacles. County opposition and government arbitrations pushed them into using the Town Development Act, but only London did so actively, since the other cities saw little organizational interest in the far-flung and random dispersal implicit in the act (random in the sense that action depended upon the distribution of willing partners). For the most part, however, the cities had to manage their extensive programs of redevelopment and new growth within boundaries that were only narrowly and grudgingly extended. Increasingly the government's arbitrations, its new town initiatives, and its sponsorship of special regional plans became the strategic determinants of local policymaking, while the ambitious city housing and development policies began simultaneously to wane for other reasons. Nonetheless, the city governments had an enormous impact upon patterns of urbanization during this period.

Stockholm offers a fascinating comparison with the big British cities. Stockholm after 1945 also had highly expansionist plans for urban growth which pivoted on the city's own powers and initiatives and were related to a massive housing program under the city's direct control. But it also had a mixture of advantages for positive planning which no British city possessed. It had considerable but less extensive problems of urban blight, and by concentrating its efforts much more upon new growth than upon redevelopment, it achieved a quicker increase in the supply of dwellings. It owned 70 percent of undeveloped land within the city and was acquiring large tracts beyond. It owned an efficient public transport system. It levied an elastic local income tax. It was surrounded not by powerful counties but by small and relatively poor communes who inevitably looked to the city for leadership in regional affairs while sometimes fearing its ambitions.

Stockholm's famous "finger plan" of city growth was based on major extensions of the subway system and the creation around each station of a neighborhood for about 10,000 people. The housing was arranged in tiered densities around the station. Groups of neighborhoods were related to a district center serving about 60,000 people. High standards of social planning prevailed, including clubs for the old, facilities for the handicapped, play centers, and other facilities to help working wives. Traffic was minimized and a network of safe walkways established. There was attention also to preserving the trees and other natural features of the landscape. A whole series of suburban townships was built along these lines (Vallingby, Farsta, and so forth), and like the English new towns they have been often admired by visitors as examples of effective public planning.[17]

Stockholm's expansion, like that of British cities, could not be stopped at its borders, however: land was needed for further satellite communities, the growing list of housing applicants had to be accommodated, public transport extended and coordinated, and other functional issues resolved. Farsighted city politicians and officials were aware of these problems from an early date, and some of them worked for the eventual "metro solution." An advisory Regional Plan Commission, staffed and led by Stockholm, was the first development. In 1957 a Greater Stockholm Planning Board was created to coordinate the location of new housing. In 1959 the government helped Stockholm by passing the Lex Bollmora which (rather like the Town Development Act in England) allowed the city to develop beyond its borders by mutual agreement to meet both its own needs and those of other communes. Ten agreements with the suburbs followed for 31,000 housing units, with 70 percent allocated to the city and 30 percent to the suburbs. A series of substantial new satellite towns grew beyond the city borders, the largest (Jarvafaltet) on government-released land for 100,000 people, and "in the process the physical shape of Stockholm for the next century was effectively determined."[18]

The process was not free from conflict by any means. The other communes resented the city's large and secret land purchases through city-owned companies (equal to 38,500 hectares by 1967). Although they sometimes welcomed a contribution from the city's building machine, they were anxious about the number of welfare cases exported from the city, wanting industrial workers instead who would contribute to the local economy. The Lex Bollmora aggravated these disagreements until in 1966 the government insisted that a common housing exchange be set up as a condition for central housing loans. As development spread, transportation conflicts also increased until in 1964 a Greater Stockholm Traffic Association was formed jointly by city and county so as to unify the ownership and planning of all public transport systems. This deal was possible only because the government agreed to pay 95 percent of the cost of new subway construction, while the city gave its transport system away virtually free of charge to the new agency.[19]

Stockholm provides a possibly unique example of the ability of a city government to integrate public transport, housing, shopping centers, social facilities, and environmental protection through a system of public land management and coordinated programs. The city plan of 1952 was never formally adopted, but it was implemented through site plans for each individual district that were worked out jointly by the politically appointed commissioners responsible for city planning, real estate, and other functions and were approved by the city council. These site plans were also the subject of architectural competitions. The city-controlled companies responsible for land assembly and cooperative housing played an essential supportive role. The only major failure over coordination concerned the decentralization of employment; for example, by 1965 Vallingby had 54 jobs for every 100 working residents, but only about half these jobs were filled by local people. This situation represented a defeat for the full ideal of "walk to work" and was caused (as in Britain) by difficulties—and eventual abandonment—of the coordination of housing lists with job vacancies. The abandonment showed that there was a limit to the "fine tuning" which the planners could accomplish, but their achievements were considerable.[20]

Why was Stockholm's planning more effective than that of British cities? In both cases, as already noted, it could be said that planning was done by a political and professional elite untrammeled by much opposition from pressure groups and able to take a broad view of civic interests. As Anton has noted, the Stockholm elite was particularly effective because of its links with the leadership of the national government. This was important because national interventions became increasingly critical as the cities expanded. The Swedish government's insistence on a common housing exchange and its financial support for the transportation agreement were critical elements in the Stockholm story. In Britain central government action was equally crucial, but no equivalent support was exercised in favor of the city governments. Instead, the national government's own initiatives, notably with respect to the new towns, played a growing part in the planning of urban growth.

At the same time, planning by these cities shows the influence of welfare goals, particularly those espoused by Labour or Social Democratic parties. It is true that city policies at this time were not based closely upon party politics; in Stockholm, as in some British cities, alternations of political leadership brought changes in policy emphasis rather than in fundamental decisions. But periods of national leadership by left-wing parties left their imprint upon city policies, as did the general postwar belief in the capacity of drastic root and branch measures to eliminate the old evils of urban squalor and poverty.

Unfortunately, the welfare goals were too narrowly or technocratically conceived in terms of improved physical standards. In the British redevelopment areas overcrowding was dramatically reduced and the physical condition and equipment of the housing greatly improved. But the resort to high-rise development in both inner areas and new suburbs (but especially, of course, in the former) was unpopular among families with children, proved in some cases to be structurally unsafe, and led to extensive vandalism. The "highrise folly" of the 1950s and 1960s, as it was subsequently widely regarded, occurred not only in Britain and Stockholm but also in the big state-supported projects around Paris like

Sarcelles, in public projects in the largest American cities, and indeed almost everywhere. High-rise development was more acceptable as a way of life on the European continent and especially in Sweden than in England, where even slums were tiny houses with back yards, but as the scale and massiveness of public housing projects grew everywhere, so did criticism of it. In Britain cities started to tear down tall housing blocks after less than twenty years' life or allocated them to students or the homeless at very low rents or wrote them off as hopelessly vandalized. The government ruled that they ought not to be occupied by families with young children, and the Greater London Council (the GLC succeeded the London County Council) declared its wish to eliminate all tall flats as quickly as possible. In St. Louis the mayor in one spectacular act bombed a vast high-rise complex out of existence.

High-rise public housing was the product of many causes, and its history is very informative about the problems and limitations of positive city planning.[21] The cities had some organizational and political interest, even under European conditions, in keeping their population as far as possible within their own boundaries. To do otherwise would have increased the city's debt load and would have reduced its political status, and there are social arguments (as noted in chapter 1) for minimizing a rapid population exodus. These were not decisive influences, however. The London County Council, because of its strong resource base, its large population, and its commitment to high housing standards, was prepared for and even enthusiastic about large-scale dispersal. The LCC was unique, but other British cities would have built more houses on their periphery instead of building high if they could have annexed more land. They were blocked by exurban and agricultural interests, while cities also came under pressure from building contractors to utilize new mass production techniques for public housing. In the United Kingdom agricultural interests influenced the central government to provide large extra subsidies for high-rise building, thus diverting or perverting the cities' "organizational interests" in this direction.

Thus the history also shows the limitations of planning by representative local elites. These elites were strongly influenced by external pressures and inducements and were also inadequately prepared to control their own officials, especially city architects, who in the spirit of Le Corbusier often welcomed the opportunities for monumental construction. Many politicians of course took a similar view, and all participants were strongly influenced by the ideology of this period. Still, history does underline the point that planning can become technocratic in a manner which is highly insensitive to a captive clientele and extremely wasteful of public resources. Even if densities needed to be kept high, this aim could have been met in ways—such as denser low-rise building or the modification of space standards for side roads, schools, and so forth—which were more acceptable to the local population.

The technocratic mistakes of postwar city planning must be set against some real achievements. Equality was furthered by extending housing and environmental benefits to numerous families who would otherwise have had to rely on "filtering upwards." The Stockholm plan, and some of the new towns in Britain, score well on the criteria of an efficient urban system and a safe, attractive public environment. Some of the early Stockholm satellites score well in terms of meeting diverse social needs, such as those of working wives, teenagers, and the old, and produce high levels of social satisfaction.[22] One can perceive here at least a brave attempt to order the physical environment according to social ideals. But instead of improving and spreading these experiments, city planning everywhere has become more tied to market forces.

Cities against Decline

Even in the more ambitious European cities, the period of vigorous urban reconstruction and growth has now ended. The big city development machines, where they existed, have run out of money, land, and political support. Almost all central cities have become introverted and preoccupied with problems of decline. Sometimes the "urban crisis" seemed to be discovered almost overnight by local and national politicians, and it led everywhere to new central government interventions and initiatives.

It is necessary to keep in mind the distinction between socioeconomic changes in the geography of cities and changes in the perceived problems and attempted remedies of city governments. Decline within the city's boundaries goes with growth within the broader region, and for this and other reasons central cities have special financial problems which influence their planning. It will be best first to consider briefly the problems of urban decline (economic, social, and financial) from a broader standpoint. Then we can evaluate the responses of city planning.

The rapid decline of manufacturing employment in the inner areas of virtually all Western cities shows the reduction of previous locational advantages such as the existence of a vast, concentrated, and varied pool of labor; abundant and often relatively cheap factory space in old premises; easy access to railheads and to docks; and links among a multitude of small firms. Modernization of factories, reliance on road transport, migration of skilled labor, new forms of communication, and increased size of firms all stimulate the exodus of some firms to new locations and the "death" of many more. The switch from manufacturing to distribution simultaneously produces new jobs in city centers, but the situations here are very various. The centers of great cities which act as headquarters for government, finance, top management, culture, and tourism, or some combination of these five activities, develop ever more specialized activities even while dispersing much routine office employment. Fair-sized regional centers tend to grow much less but also to disperse less activity, while other city centers experience stagnation or decline due to the collapse of their economic base in industry or transportation or to being bypassed as a regional center by a larger city. Among British cities, London, Manchester, and Liverpool illustrate these three situations.[23]

From a regional standpoint these locational shifts can be in many ways beneficial. The dispersed industries and labor force will enjoy better working and living conditions, which is why they have moved, especially if planning can reduce the tendencies to urban scatter and long journeys to work. Within the city, densities will be reduced and room can be found, if the environment is sufficiently improved, for some white-collar commuters to live closer to their work in the city center and to its cultural facilities. If planning is intelligent enough to realize these opportunities, there will still be transitional problems of unemployment and poverty within the city. If economic change is very rapid, and if the city's employment base declines faster than its population, then these problems will be sudden and severe.

Just this situation has come about in many cities. Initially and until 1945 or later, population was moving out from cities faster than employment, led by middle-class commuters who often continued to work in the city center. After 1945 the exodus of employment accelerated steadily, sometimes as in Britain, with the active support of public policy. This development was welcomed by planners as facilitating a more balanced dispersal process, especially to planned developments like new towns; but in the 1960s and 1970s employment contracted rapidly in the inner urban areas not only (or primarily) because of continued dispersal but because of the deaths of many firms which could not survive under much changed locational and technological conditions. The relative decline of employment was most severe in the United States; between 1960 and 1970, ten of the largest central cities lost an average 6.8 percent of population but 10.6 percent of jobs, and after 1970 loss of manufacturing jobs accelerated fast.[24]

The powerful functions of the "world cities" renders them much more resistant to economic decline. Plans for London and Paris in the mid-

1960s still diagnosed the existence of an overconcentration of employment, since a rapid fall in manufacturing was offset both by population loss and the growth of offices and services. Only a few years later the Greater London Council was ringing alarm bells about London's prosperity, although in fact the employment and economic position of London remains much stronger than that of other British cities. The bankruptcy of New York City may suggest how vulnerable to depression a world city can be, but New York's central area remains prosperous and still expanding, and its fiscal crisis had special as well as general causes. Other cities resistant to decline include those with relatively small old urban cores, such as some in the American west and southwest; these are also the cities within the United States that are most successful in annexing new territory, a solution no longer open to the big old eastern and midwestern cities.

Social change has both followed and preceded these economic shifts. In the old working-class areas, especially those that have been comprehensively replanned, there has been a sharp population decline that is reflected by a dramatic fall in the size of the average household. Consequently there is much less overcrowding, but the selective nature of the urban exodus has accentuated the numbers of old and dependent people and has eroded traditional kinship ties. There are fewer shopping and commercial facilities and low private investment. But simultaneously many inner areas have been colonized by immigrants or minority ethnic groups with strong kinship ties, high birth rates, and expanding numbers, who recreate problems of overcrowding and introduce new problems of youthful unemployment and teenage crime. Finally, in some inner areas middle-class groups have been persuaded to live in the city through infiltration and the improvement of habitats with potential environmental charm or quality. The juxtaposition of these different kinds of community within inner areas produces both social conflicts, relating to housing, for example, and sometimes a degree of mutual support ("gentrification" raises income and investment levels).

There are, again, great differences between cities of a social kind. The enormous black communities of American cities, sometimes now approaching a majority, as in Chicago or Detroit, have no close parallel in Europe; and the suburban resistance to their outward spread adds to employment deficiencies within the city. In Germany and other European continental countries, the oldest inner city areas are increasingly occupied by migrant workers who stay only a few years, and in Britain more permanent immigrant groups occupy similar areas. The populations are smaller than in the United States, but housing and sometimes employment problems are similar. Gentrification is most marked in the great world cities such as London and Paris and is less apparent in old industrial cities. But in the inner areas of these world cities, a polarization of social classes also occurs. In Paris the better arrondissements to the west of the city are increasingly monopolized by professional and managerial groups, while "foreigners" are concentrated in the areas with most unemployment to the north and northeast.[25] In London there are clear contrasts between the depopulated, traditional working-class areas of the East End, where there has been extensive redevelopment, and ethnic minorities living in crowded conditions in large dilapidated houses to the northwest; but there are also spreading islands of gentrification in boroughs like Islington or Battersea, and it is in the mixed boroughs that local politics are most vigorous.[26]

The financial problems of cities are a product of high costs with complex causes. In general the costs of city governments rise with size and density of population. Explanations include the high costs of public land acquisition and renewal of the urban fabric in dense inner areas; high costs of traffic regulation, building code enforcement, and police and fire services in such areas; and high costs of welfare expenditure on personal social services, housing, and sometimes income support. (In many North American cities welfare payments are still partially a local responsibility, but in European countries they are usually nationalized and standardized.) In addition, the higher staffing ratios found in big cities are only partly due to the provision of more specialized services and often reflect political and bureaucratic pressures for "payroll padding." The former pressure is aimed at providing jobs for the unemployed; the latter seems a function of size and the power of public service unions. Both pressures contributed to New York City's bankruptcy. In Europe, city governments are often more insulated from political, although not from bureaucratic, pressures for the growth of public employment.[27]

These high costs of big cities have historically been balanced by high local tax revenues generated by property values and by the above-average incomes of big city residents. The higher incomes used to be explained by the greater productivity of labor in large urban concentrations. This superior productivity is no longer so evident, and in any event is now usually spread over a much broader area than the city itself, so that average incomes in the city fall sometimes below the national average. Once again variations are considerable, depending upon urban boundaries, the extent to which richer people have fled the city (or are returning), and the wealth of the city center. A world city like London still has above average incomes as well as property values in the central area exceeding those of the whole of Scotland. Generally cities which perform major financial functions in a national or world setting have the most resilient base of property taxation.

Some of the costs of decline which worry a city government, such as the higher burden of debt and the difficulties of staff redundancies, are artificial from a regional standpoint. In the long run, a smaller population requires reduced services, and its lower density should mean lower average costs. But the problems are more serious if the urban exodus is removing wealthier citizens while welfare costs in the city are rising, which is often the case, most of all in the United States.

What responses have cities made to these problems? One universal policy since the war has been the redevelopment of city centers. In the United States this policy was seen as an essential protection of the city's economic base against the forces of dispersal and the unrestricted competition of suburban and out-of-town shopping centers. Federal aid for urban redevelopment was channeled for this purpose. Highway money was freely spent for improving access by road users to the city center. Some dramatic office and commercial redevelopments resulted, and some centers were revitalized. For example, in Pittsburgh the bold new skyscrapers in the Golden Triangle were combined with new cultural facilities and the elimination of the city's pall of smog. But high economic and social costs were also associated with the policies adopted, such as the increase in traffic congestion, the rundown of public transport, and the disturbances that the new roads and traffic brought the residents of surrounding areas. The contrast between the financially cossetted city center and the decayed and neglected areas surrounding it became more striking. The enhanced property values in the center were needed to pay the city payroll, the welfare checks, and the social services, but otherwise there was little common interest and frequently little contact between the commuters to the center and the residents of surrounding ghettos. The relationship between them was increasingly characterized by financial dependence rather than by complementary needs or lifestyles. With automation and the decline of traditional small industries, the workers living around the city center became less essential to its functioning.

In Britain and Europe, the slower growth in the number of cars and stronger planning powers provided greater protection to the city centers against the forces of dispersal. The postwar rebuilding of bombed areas was executed through comprehensive municipal land assembly and redevelopment and introduced some innovations, such as the extensive walkways of Rotterdam or Coventry, but much in these schemes was traditional and conventional. The London County Council worked to protect theaters, historic buildings, and some residential areas against the incursion of new offices and restricted the number of tall buildings on aesthetic grounds; these policies, although only partially successful, also paid off economically with the subsequent tourist boom. London, however, was one partial exception to urban policies, which generally put modernization of commercial buildings and road layouts first. Many British cities, such as Birmingham or Nottingham, encircled their centers tightly with new ring roads which were ruthlessly cut through dense areas. As in the United States, redevelopment was usually executed in partnership with private developers, but the city's interest was often narrowly interpreted in terms of traffic and road requirements, with municipal or cultural buildings or a small open space occasionally added. In most European countries, such projects have tended to become more narrowly functional and architecturally bare under the pressure of private profit margins, and while internal layouts are more efficient, there is less social as well as visual diversity in the city's buildings and facilities. The modernization schemes have been strongly criticized by urban sociologists in France and elsewhere, who often view them as the final stage of neocapitalist development. Centers with attractive old buildings and townscapes capable of preservation have grown in popularity, and some cities have reaped the advantage of conservation policies or of simple delay in pursuing modernization proposals.

In Britain and some other European countries, planning powers were firmly used to protect city centers against competing developments. This policy was only possible in Britain because counties and the central government took much the same view as the cities themselves. Consequently out-of-town shopping centers and other types of scattered facilities were usually prohibited; for example, Haydock Park, a major greenfield dovolopmont at tho junction of two motorwayo in Lancoohiro woo rejected because of its probable effects upon the city centers of Liverpool and Manchester. Recently, however, these restrictions have been considerably relaxed.

Because of the fixation upon the city center, there was little attempt to promote the development of major subcenters which could cater in an integrated manner to the needs of an increasingly dispersed population. Such developments have occurred sometimes in spite of rather than because of general planning, as in the case of the large suburban center at Croydon (twelve miles from central London), which the local borough initiated in defiance of the London plan. In Paris regional and city plans now provide for concentrating resources upon developing some large suburban subcenters, but the first of these (La Défense) is primarily an extension of the central area's office complex helped by a new subway. There are cases where cities acted more progressively, as with Stockholm's at least partial success with district centers; and the case for a more balanced system of urban centers is increasingly recognized.

The biggest differences in city planning policies concerned the treatment of the extensive areas of urban blight, bad housing, and overcrowded populations. In Britain, as already noted, many of these areas have been completely rebuilt and the local population rehoused locally or in new developments. In the United States the federal Housing Act of 1949 proclaimed similar goals of eliminating slums and assuring a decent home and a suitable living environment for every American family, but the act and its successors produced quite different effects. Cities could assemble land by compulsory acquisition and could resell lots for housing, commercial, or institutional purposes. The cities' "organizational interest" in using the act was strong because the federal government paid two-thirds of the cost and the city contribution could be paid in the form of local public works which might be needed anyhow. But reliance on the participation of private developers, or of large institutions such as hospitals and universities, meant that sites must be selected to meet the developers' needs, and also that existing residents had little hope of paying the rents of the new residential apartments.

By 1965, 1,560 renewal projects had been approved in 750 cities, $4 billion voted in federal funds, and forty-two square miles of land approved for acquisition. Compared with redevelopment in Britain, U.S. renewal areas were relatively small—for example, only 1 percent of land in New York City was acquired during twenty-five years. Still, the impact of the program was very considerable. Its justification was that it enabled cities to revive their economic and cultural life; for example, Lincoln Center was built in New York, downtown Boston was restored, universities and hospitals were helped to expand, and richer residents and some jobs were attracted back to the cities. Urban renewal could therefore be viewed as a counterweight to the encouragement that federal housing and highway subsidies had given urban dispersal. It might have been simpler—and it certainly would have been cheaper—to reverse the assistance to dispersal.

Urban renewal displaced (because of developers' interests) large numbers of relatively poor people from dwellings which were sometimes in good condition; 41 percent of the dwellings in the clearance area of the Italian West End in Boston were so described. Such egregious decisions resembled the technocratic mistakes of European city planners. But the effects were far worse because hardly any public housing was built for those displaced, compensation to help relocation was small, and the total supply of low-rent dwellings was much reduced. The effects were therefore to spread and probably to intensify slum conditions, not to eliminate them. Equality and welfare goals were subordinated to the organizational interest of cities in raising property values.

This interest may even so have been misleading because cities had later to pick up the checks for deteriorating areas of blight.[28]

In the 1960s, the idea that physical renewal could solve the cities' problems became discredited. Instead, in the United States, and later in Britain, under the pressure of race riots and social tensions, governments focused their attentions upon the notion of "multiple social deprivations" among the urban poor. Subsequently their attentions switched to economic disabilities of unemployment and low incomes, which were seen by some critics as the fundamental causes of urban problems. Finally, city planners were urged to tackle all three problems—physical decay, social deprivations, and economic decline—through comprehensive plans, or a "total" approach. Simultaneously governments urged the need for greater public participation to ascertain the needs and overcome the alienation of urban inhabitants, and they also tried to pinpoint their financial support upon the areas of greatest deprivation.

In the United States President Kennedy's Economic Opportunity Act (1964) bypassed the local government structure in its aim of achieving the "maximum feasible participation" of the citizens of deprived areas. The special local agencies set up to disburse federal assistance coopted radical black leaders into the governmental process, but the difficulties of grass-roots participation and evidence of corruption or misuse of funds combined with the hostility of city governments to discredit and abolish the programs.[29]

President Johnson's model cities legislation (1966) worked through city governments and introduced the notion of a comprehensive but selective and experimental approach to the improvement of specified neighborhoods. The cities were free to propose what measures they liked (economic, social, or physical) but had to comply with close federal guidelines intended to support comprehensive planning, "extensive" public participation, and concentration on the worst areas. This program was extended under congressional pressure to 147 local governments instead of the few cities originally intended to receive more concentrated assistance, and the funds spent were also much less than intended because of the failure of many federal agencies, despite presidential urging, to contribute to the program. Nonetheless, federal requirements enabled mayors to resist the wishes of many city councils to spread the available aid more widely, and the program thereby contributed on a modest scale to welfare and equality goals.[30]

Subsequent American policies have moved away from detailed federal interventions in cities in favor of general-purpose assistance governed by broad and loose planning requirements. The 1974 Housing and Community Development Act rolled up seven federal support programs, including urban renewal and model cities, into a single community development block grant (CDBG). This grant was allocated on a formula based on statistics of population, overcrowding in houses, and poverty (the last counting twice), but its application was limited by a "hold-harmless" arrangement for phasing out existing grant entitlements slowly. Federal aid was spread very broadly among cities, and cities won back very considerable freedom in how they used the money. Public participation is still required but is defined by the city. Aid is no longer funneled into particular neighborhoods. An important innovation is that each local government must prepare a housing assistance plan showing how it will meet the needs of low- or moderate-income families who are "expected to reside" in their areas. This clause quickly raised a court case about the failure of nine suburbs to plan housing for the "overspill" of poor people from the central city (Hartford, Connecticut), which echoed European conflicts. In general, however, the act's administration confirms Beer's description of a victory by "topocrats" (local mayors or governors) over "technocrats" (the professionals in Washington), although there are still strong pressures in Congress for establishing stronger federal controls over urban policies.[31]

In Britain the government's urban program of 1968 represented a pale and staid reflection of American ideas at the very time when American political opinion was shifting away from them. An interdepartmental committee administered a very modest fund (£70 million spent over ten years) paid out mainly to city governments for spending in their poorest areas; the main effect was to speed slightly the normal development of social services, primarily nursery schools and child care. There were also small experiments in local action research (the community development programs, or CDPs), but the mainly radical researchers concluded that what local people wanted or needed was not social aid but more jobs and better incomes, so that (they claimed) strong government action would be required to keep industry in inner areas. The CDPs were terminated in 1976. Another pale reflection of American policy consisted in government-commissioned experimental studies of possible comprehensive policies for fighting urban decline; they mainly revealed a complete diversity of diagnosis and prescription. In some ways this discovery was useful—it at least pointed to the variety of conditions to be found within inner areas.[32]

In 1977 the Labour government embarked upon more detailed measures of urban assistance. The minister (Mr. Shore) argued that past planning policies had run down urban economies and that dispersal from cities ought to be halted. The government offered a new though still modest package of aid to selected inner urban areas, with particular stress upon land acquisition, cheap loans, and grants for industrial buildings or conversions. Moreover, "partnership committees" comprising both ministers and local councillors were established for seven areas, with the intention of coordinating and pinpointing the programs of central and local departments. The Conservative government of 1979 is likely both to reduce aid and to restore more local responsibility.

Despite the exhortations about "total planning," the physical renewal of urban areas remains a prime objective. In the United States the redevelopment legislation was supplemented from 1954 onward by policies of piecemeal rehabilitation using a mixture of methods (building code enforcement, federal mortgage insurance for black homeowners, subsidies for low-income tenants, house improvement grants). The 1974 act signaled a return to these policies, with more stress upon the connections between planning and housing, but the neighborhoods being upgraded with CDBG money are not necessarily the most blighted—they are more likely to be areas judged capable of significant improvement. The worst city areas remain affected by cumulative blight and often by arson, dereliction, and abandonment.

In Britain, the policy switch came more slowly as local authorities clung to their faith in wholesale demolition and replacement. The 1969 Housing Act established "general improvement areas" in which local authorities had powers to buy land, give improvement grants to house owners or rehabilitate housing themselves, and make environmental improvements. Conservation areas could also be designated for protecting and repairing fine areas of townscape. Housing programs were diversified by government aid to cooperatives. Under these programs the worst urban areas have been much less neglected than in the United States. For example, the East End of Glasgow, perhaps the most blighted urban area in Britain, is the subject of a very ambitious and costly partnership scheme between central and local government, and to help with its finance a new town already designated in the Clyde region (Stonehouse) was peremptorily abandoned. City efforts and expenditure upon rehabilitation and conservation have been considerable, but private investment within the blighted areas has largely dried up except for house improvements by owner occupiers, and the provision or maintenance of rented housing is becoming almost a monopoly of local government. This situation strains local finance severely and leads to long delays in the use of sites and buildings.

National governments have also, as noted, placed increasing weight upon planning and participation procedures. In the United States, starting with the 1954 Housing Act, federal grants have become conditional upon the preparation both of local community plans and of overall metropolitan plans so as to concert local policies, but the planning requirement has in practice been a rather flimsy constraint except for special programs like model cities. As I have noted, public participation is now left more to local discretion, but in fact there is considerable participation—not in deprived areas, but on a broad citywide basis—over community development programs. In Britain a 1968 act required the larger local governments to prepare broad-based "structure plans" on which local plans are based. The minister must be satisfied that the authority has sounded out public opinion over the plan's provisions, and the structure plan itself is then the subject of a public examination when general arguments for as well as against the plan can be put by citizen groups. The difficulty is that these exercises, while generally conscientiously performed, concern broad schemes whose impact is often obscure to the individual citizen; those participating are either closely interested parties or the more sophisticated voluntary organizations. There have, however, been some efforts by professional planners to consult residents affected by a particular scheme directly, but often this device is judicially difficult (if there is a subsequent local inquiry) and unpopular with elected representatives.[33]

The principle of central government aid to cities in trouble has to compete with the claims of other local governments and the swings of national politics. Special urban programs, where they exist, contribute a very small proportion of total government aid. In 1970 total federal aid per person was actually slightly lower for central cities ($50.68) than for local government generally ($52.25).[34] Any basic financial shift turns on redistributing the large functional grants (such as highways), or the large general-purpose grants such as revenue sharing and the CDBG in the United States or the rate support grant in Britain (equal to £6,000 million in 1978). In Britain a Labour government adjusted the formula for rate support grants to favor cities, but the Conservatives reversed the position to favor counties. In the United States Democratic presidents favor cities which provide much of their political support, but Republican ones favor suburbs and prefer to work through state, not city, governments. City governments cannot rely simply on the politics of grantsmanship but have to devise and press for planning policies which can help their condition.

The Appraisal of City Plans

City planning, it is clear, cannot be divorced from the framework of national legislation, policies, subsidies, and interventions. In their expansionist phase, the most successful cities depended upon the strong powers and financial support furnished by helpful governments. The nature of this support also influenced the character of their planning; for example, the era of high-rise building by cities in Britain owed a lot to a housing subsidy system which placed upon the national exchequer almost all the extra cost of building high. The problems of urban decline have brought an increase in the frequency, volatility, and specificity of national interventions. Cities appear to have become more open, both politically and financially, to such interventions. Where they resisted this process and regained more autonomy, as in the United States, they also seem more vulnerable to the forces of decline.

At the same time, in most democracies it is the cities as operating authorities who make detailed plans and policies within the national guidelines. The national policymakers cannot know or foresee how their general policy aims will be interpreted by cities, and their detailed interventions usually take the form of powers of review or arbitration, not direct initiatives. Moreover, many of the problems of cities stem from conflicts of interest within the urban region which no authority is competent to resolve. Cities have sometimes followed policies which are plainly inconsistent with or are unrelated to the aims of a regional plan favored by central government, but the city has been too strong or regional planning too weak for a reconciliation of goals. The planning problems of cities have been a major reason for the introduction of "metro schemes," discussed in the next chapter, but the metro authorities can complicate as well as attempt to resolve regional issues. Policymaking within the urban region represents a complicated jigsaw in which the roles of participating governments interact, so that an account of city planning is necessarily to some extent an abstraction from this broader survey.

Both national and local policies have also to be understood in the context of economic and social change and of changing beliefs and ideologies. A full explanation of these influences lies beyond the scope of this book, but their impact upon city planning has been very marked. In the first postwar phase, major schemes of physical development and reconstruction were assumed to be intrinsically desirable. Much of the accumulated structure of the city was judged ripe for replacement, and progress was on the side of the bulldozer. The same solutions to urban problems were favored in different countries at the same time. In the 1950s vast projects of high-rise housing seemed the obvious solution to the massive housing demands stimulated by slum clearance, rapidly falling household size, and welfare policies. In the 1960s, massive highway building in the cities which had proceeded rapidly in the United States became for a time the orthodox reaction in Europe to new problems of expanding car ownership and traffic congestion. President Pompidou threw his weight behind a Right Bank motorway for Paris, and Prime Minister Heath declared that "we must care for the motorist." This was the period when cities planned and partly built a hierarchical system of new roads and put road modernization high on their objectives for city centers. But within quite a short time these policies had become widely doubted or rejected. Urban problems were quickly redefined and perceived in new ways.

In the more recent phase of planning, surgical operations upon the city's body have fallen out of favor. The aims have become piecemeal adaptation, rehabilitation, or conservation of the urban fabric—described sometimes as "soft" instead of "hard" planning. What accounts for this policy change? One reason is greater stringency of city finances, often combined with a reduced tempo of business enterprise. Then, too, there is the growing opposition of environmental groups to new developments and social criticism of the actual effects of public road and housing projects. There may also be more subtle causes for the opinion swing from belief in technological progress to cultural (and perhaps political) conservatism.

All city governments have experienced the impact of these policy changes. The main differences between them concern the ideological and political realm—in how far they have attempted to plan, manage, and direct change. This difference was naturally clearest in the expansionist period, when the results of strong municipal initiative and comprehensive planning in a city like Stockholm contrasted sharply with American cities, where the interests of private development dominated and public policies were poorly coordinated. But in the latter phase also, conservation and rehabilitation policies have been welded into a strong coordinated strategy by some European cities—Stockholm is again an example—but not by others.

Planners themselves have been accused by some critics of causing the problems of urban decline. They have done so, it is said, by insisting upon separating land uses, reducing densities, and encouraging the dispersal of people and firms, thus destroying the closeknit and varied pattern of activities typical of old urban cores. Still, antiplanners such as Jane Jacobs[35] considerably overstate the attractions of these old cores, which also contain large homogeneous zones of bad housing and poor environmental conditions that have for long provided the stimulus to steady migration. It is true that planners have insufficiently recognized the value of diversified uses of attractive old centers, although public planning can also be the necessary instrument for saving such areas from the bulldozers of private developers.

It is not clear that the planned dispersal policies of European cities have been mistaken in principle—on the contrary, they may not prove adequate for stabilizing the population in acceptable environmental conditions. Out-migration has been almost as rapid in American as in

British cities, despite suburban opposition to the arrival of blacks. In New York City this has not been the case, and the population has remained at close to 8 million people, while Greater London declined drastically from 8 to 6½ million, but the employment and social problems in the inner areas of New York have also proved to be more severe. The London greenbelt and the reduction of densities have at least helped to retain the city's character as a series of relatively open and distinctive townships, the "unique city" so admired by Rasmussen.[36]

Where European planners often went wrong was in forcing the pace of change too much and in undertaking insensitive or monumental rebuilding plans. More use of housing rehabilitation, and smaller and more socially mixed public housing projects, would have softened changes in community structure and would have given redevelopment a more human face. Small industrial firms were too easily regarded as dispensable instead of being helped to survive. Planners should have given more priority to establishing good locations and incentives for local shopping centers, new commercial development, and the provision of social facilities. Planning in fact called for sensitive treatment of the microscale of land uses and activities in inner areas. Instead, cities like Liverpool or Glasgow wrapped up their resources in big housing projects and great new roads and interchanges, leaving areas of derelict land with no profitable use in prospect. The fault in such cases was not excessive dispersal but the attempt to replan the city on a scale which was not financially viable or socially acceptable. In the process, too, the meaning of local community was lost.

Some economic and social problems cannot be solved by city governments even with generous financial assistance. The traditional diversity of big city economies gives more scope for regeneration there than in other depressed zones, but some of the conditions of regeneration are harder to provide—for example, it is often difficult to find suitable housing or housing land for skilled workers, and if roads are built for the modern requirements of industry, environmental conditions deteriorate, and the roads may be used in the end mainly by commuters to the city center. The city has the continuous problem of reconciling conflict between its economic base and its environmental capacity. Often the answer may lie in developing the city's role as a major service center, transforming the inner areas gradually to provide a satisfactory living environment for more of the workers in the central area. At the same time industry on a smaller scale can still be fostered by developing the city's special advantages for this purpose. But substantial transformations cannot be avoided, and environmental capacity provides a limiting factor which can be tested empirically by observing the propensity to flee the city's domain.

The goals of long-term planning in cities have been obscured and distorted by the pressures for quick action to solve urgent problems of unemployment and deprivation. These problems cannot be written off as simply transitional, but they do to some extent represent a concentration of human casualties of change who require the special attention of national policymakers. This is the justification for increased government intervention in the affairs of cities, but such interference will hardly help cities if they try to put the clock back in the immediate interest of victims. A return to the high-density, industrialized city is not practicable, and the policies that the notion demands would probably be self-defeating. The confusion of directions in city policies shows up blatantly in the planning documents of recent years. The growing stalemate over city policies seems to call for more socially sensitive and economically realistic planning which can avoid the perversion of a narrow concept of organizational interest.

This perversion, however, is likely to occur if the financial and structural basis of local government forces cities into a narrow interpretation of their interests. Many problems of urban planning and of urban finance can today be tackled only upon a regional basis. They require policies which can relate the still rapid changes on the urban frontier to the sensitive and difficult adaptations which are required within the urban core and which can share costs and benefits more equitably between the various parts of the urban region. They require actions by central or state governments to create an organizational and financial framework adequate for such purposes.

3: Metro Government and Urban Planning

The Case for Metro Schemes

If cities can no longer plan effectively, then the obvious remedy is local government reform. Reform movements have increasingly centered upon what are known in the United States as "metro schemes,"[1] although other countries have most fully developed such schemes. Basically a metro scheme brings local government structure into line with social and economic realities by recognizing the many inter-dependencies and joint functional interests which exist in a great urban area. This is done by setting up an overall public authority for the entire area.

Metro theories reject the concept of simply expanding the boundaries of a major city because this course is assumed to be politically impracticable and democratically undesirable—at any rate for big urban areas with populations of perhaps a million or more. A million is an arbitrary figure—it was suggested by the English Royal Commission on Local Government but backed by no evidence.[2] Consequently a metro authority shares powers with smaller local governments within its area. This strengthens the political appeal of a metro scheme because if necessary the existing local governments can be left undisturbed or only reorganized at a later stage, as happened in Metro Toronto. Again, the structure of the metro authority itself can vary. If it is no more than a coordinating committee of the other local governments with no or very few executive powers, then it is a step toward metro government rather than its achievement. Metro governments proper have substantial direct powers and, if they are to form part of a democratic system of local government, must be elected indirectly from leaders of smaller units or directly by citizens at large or through some mixture of the two. Indirect election eases the political transition. Direct election confers more authority and greater independence over policy formulation which may, however, be negated by stronger resistance to the policies.

It will be useful to start by reviewing five issues about the desirability of metro systems.

1. *Competition and Equality.* Some American writers justify a fragmented local government system on the grounds that it gives citizens a choice between the different bundle of services and taxes offered by each unit. A citizen can choose his place of residence partly at least on this basis.[3] One weakness of this theory is that local government units are shaped by political history and cannot usually grow or shrink like business firms by competitive action. Moreover the local services provided are correlated mainly with the wealth of an area and are probably only a minor factor in individuals' choice of residence. Freedom of choice over local government services will still occur among the various local units under a metro scheme. It is sometimes one objective of such a scheme to establish a greater equality of size and resources among the local units, which avoids the disparate type of competition between very large and very small units.

A metro system will in theory promote equity. It can take over functions such as large transportation, recreational, and cultural facilities which have broad catchment areas and others such as social welfare which have a very uneven incidence of need. Additionally the metro body can operate a system of financial equalization for the benefit of its poorer and needier units. Financial equalization may of course be operated anyhow by a central or state government and possibly with more political impartiality than a metro authority would show in practice; but the metro body should have greater local knowledge and accountability, together with the possibility of linking its support with other objectives and of switching flexibly between financial aid and service provision.

2. *Community and Lifestyles.* Questions about the structure of local communities and their lifestyles have become increasingly significant for local government. Neighborhood values have been rediscovered both as a source of social satisfaction and as a means of political action. Territorial organizations have become important as the best way of protecting the local environment or of procuring better public services. Suburban amenity societies flourish, and in the inner city, action groups are formed to resist unwanted developments and to demand new facilities. The growing importance of ethnicity as the basis for choice of residence and the greater self-consciousness of ethnic groups, particularly in the United States,[4] increases tensions between territorial groups. The widespread attempts of governments (both central and local) to develop public participation in planning have also stimulated local action groups and have increased the political significance of localized communities.

There are, however, large differences in the effectiveness of local political action, which reflect the stability and homogeneity as well as the wealth, education, and access to political power of the local residents. This point can be seen most clearly not in city-suburban conflicts but in conflicts among suburban jurisdictions. Because of the specialization of housing markets and the effects of upward mobility, many suburbs are relatively transient places where organization is weak compared with the rich suburbs, whose residents have finally "arrived."

These local community pressures cut two ways. On the one hand they suggest the democratic advantage of very localized units, but on the other they reveal (again) the inequalities which flow from the localization of power. This tension is relevant for the allocation of functions. Oliver Williams draws a distinction between technical, or "system-maintenance," services such as transportation and water supplies, which can reasonably be centralized, and "lifestyle" services such as education, local planning, and perhaps police protection, which should remain localized.[5] But a service which is "technical" to one person affects another's lifestyle. Few things could have had a bigger impact on the lifestyles of the residents of East Boston than the development of Logan airport, for example,[6] and roads and public transport everywhere have a powerful differential impact upon local life and environment. Conversely, lifestyle services often have a system-maintenance function; for example, local planning should relate to the functioning of the whole urban area, and local police services have obvious "externalities" in an age of mobile criminals. Although doubtless there are differences of impact, it would seem that most public services involve political and social issues which transcend the local level.

Consequently it can be argued that the best way to recognize both the local and the metropolitan significance of a service is to divide it between two levels of government in a logical manner. Examples of such divisions are main highways and local streets; main drainage and local sewers; refuse disposal and refuse collection; rapid transit and local buses; big and little parks or cultural centers; higher education and basic education; hospitals and health clinics; big and small redevelopment or housing projects; and so on. Metro systems can recognize the geographical and political logic of these functional divisions, which correspond to differences in scale and externalities between the functioning of a locality and of a large urban system and to the different political interests of the smaller and larger urban community.

On the other hand the concept of metropolitan-local division of a wide range of functions meets with arguments for integrated functional management. The concentration of a whole function (or as much of it as possible) in the same hands should simplify coordination and reduce boundary frictions within the service in question (although it may weaken coordination *between* services). It will thereby pinpoint organizational and political responsibility for the service. In the case of education and personal health and welfare services, professional pressures often strongly back the case for integration.

Thus the issues of functional allocation under a metro scheme raise the familiar issue of the conflict between areal coordination (implying functional splits) and functional coordination (weakening areal coordination). Metro schemes give variable answers to this problem, sometimes dividing or sharing some function between the two levels, sometimes concentrating a whole function at one or the other level. How this equation works out varies both with different functional pressures and, also very significantly, with the political and organizational weight accorded to (or accumulated by) each governmental level. A metro scheme may be top-heavy, bottom-heavy, or more or less balanced. It may also accord more or less well with the logic of a dual level of functional responsibilities which is to some extent intrinsic to the metro concept. Theoretically speaking, the resolution of these issues depends upon the values ascribed to efficiency, community, and equality, which were discussed in chapter 1.

3. *Area and Functions.* In the United States the theme of "small and large together"[7] has gained ground. This theory would combine a large metro government with small local units, so as (one hopes) to mix the advantages of both concepts. The theory could also imply breaking down the structure of big city government into smaller units. The problem is to determine *how* small these units should be. If the metro scheme as a whole is to be bottom-heavy or evenly balanced, then the second-tier units must have the minimum size and resources necessary for functional efficiency. There is plenty of argument about the necessary size, but the London reform, for example, was premised on the basis that a local borough needed about 250,000 population if it was to operate strong powers, especially in the locally important services of education, health, and welfare.[8] Smaller size implies fewer powers. As units become smaller they correspond better with community feeling but can expect few public powers and may function wholly or mainly as advisory bodies and pressure groups upon higher levels of government. This result is indeed what some reformers intend, and was recommended for England by a royal commission.[9] Still, the implication for metro schemes would seem to be acceptance of *three* levels of local government.

These dilemmas of local government cannot be avoided through any system. As a general approach the "small and large" theme seems to have virtue. Its practical difficulties are illustrated perhaps by the study of citizen attitudes toward reform in four areas sponsored by the Department of Housing and Urban Development in the United States. Interestingly, in each area an elected metro was favored with functions which included transportation, water resource planning, sewerage, solid waste disposal, and metropolitan and land use planning, and also in some cases regional parks and cultural facilities, main drainage and flood control, and the coordination of personal social services. In no case, however, was the abolition of existing local governments proposed, although advisory neighborhood councils were recommended by local leaders in three of the four areas.[10]

4. *Efficiency and Planning.* A favorite argument for reform notes the economies of scale and technical efficiency which an integrated local government should be able to achieve. Clearly there are such gains, most obviously in relation to large-scale infrastructure or bulk facilities or where artificial boundaries inflate costs (as with police and fire services to some extent). But often the gains are problematic—particularly for personal services, where the advantages of employing more specialists are heavily offset by the loss of personal contacts and problems of coordination. The arguments for scale and specialization have been heavily oversold by professional associations and experts. There are considerable diseconomies of scale also, as might be inferred from the high expenditure per head of large units.[11]

Experience with metro or other reform schemes tends to confirm these doubts, because there is little evidence of overall cost savings. After the London reform, local government expenditure per head within London grew at a faster rate than for the country as a whole. But of course the improvement in services may have been relatively greater. The London evidence suggests that reform triggered off the ambitions of the councillors and officers of the new London boroughs for developing and improving services.[12]

A stronger argument for metro schemes is the value of overall planning related to the functional problems of the urban region. As the general theme of the book, this argument needs no development here, but its relevance to metro schemes will be further explored in the next two sections.

5. *Democracy and Accountability.* If local government remains fragmented, then the responsibility for dealing with broader urban problems passes inescapably to central or state governments. This result seems to represent a failure of democratic accountability as traditionally understood. Starting with the concept of civic self-government, it is logical to deduce that larger elective bodies become necessary as cities expand. The countertheory is that urbanization has become so amorphous as to defeat the construction of viable political institutions and so extensive as to become the primary responsibility of state governments (where such

exist) or of regional bodies answerable primarily to central governments. It can also be argued that metro government will not be democratic in its actual effects if it increases electoral confusion or indifference and opens up government still more to the influence of special interests.

Metro systems rest upon the geographic logic of democratic responsibility. As such they have to solve problems of functional division and of political conflict and apathy, which I will give further attention. Still, the democratic argument for a metro authority remains logical and strong in its own terms, provided it corresponds to a genuine arena of common problems and interests.[13]

Metro Schemes in Action

As cities have faced increasing social and economic problems of change and adaptation, reformers' dreams have been at least partly realized through experiments in local government reorganization. Metro schemes have been pioneered in the great urban concentrations of London, Toronto, and Stockholm and have subsequently been applied more widely in Britain, France, Canada, and other countries. The effects of these three pioneer schemes upon urban planning are the subject of this section.

The origins of the three initial metro schemes have influenced their subsequent working. Metro Toronto (1953) emerged from attempts by the city of Toronto to annex its surrounding municipalities, which caused the Ontario Municipal Board, a permanent review body, to propose, and the provincial government to accept, an alternative plan of federation. This left the city and the twelve suburban municipalities intact but created an indirectly elected Metro Council composed of twelve city representatives and the twelve suburban mayors with the first chairman (a strong personality) appointed by the provincial government to set the experiment in action. The case for some financial equalization between municipalities and for some overall direction during a period of explosive growth were major factors in the scheme's design and acceptability. Several subsequent reforms have been prompted by the reports of two one-man royal commissions and by changes in provincial-local relations. These have strengthened financial equalization, have shifted new powers to Metro (notably for welfare), have merged the suburban municipalities into only five units, have adjusted representation in favor of the growing suburbs, and have recently involved attempts to establish direction election to Metro. Despite considerable criticism and opposition, Metro Toronto has remained in existence and has adapted in some respects to the pressures for change.[14]

The Greater London Reform (1963) was wanted by hardly any of the hundred or so local authorities in this area but was enacted by a Conservative government on the advice of a royal commission. The commission put much stress upon the functional needs of urban planning and transportation and upon the argument that London comprised a single great city. The Conservatives were glad to see the end of the London County Council, a powerful, welfare-minded, and Labour-dominated authority which effectively ruled Victorian inner London; Labour naturally opposed reform but accepted the result when the first Greater London Council turned out to have a Labour majority. Unlike Metro Toronto, all the old units except for the ancient and small City of London were abolished, and in their place were put a directly elected Greater London Council and thirty-two directly elected London boroughs formed by mergers of previous units. Concurrent powers for many functions, especially for planning and housing, were given to both levels of government. From the start a question mark hung over the role of the GLC; was it, as the first councillors and officials tended to suppose, to act like an enlarged LCC, or should it adjust to a more limited, "strategic" type of role? And what would such a role imply? Since its inception few formal changes have occurred in the London scheme, but the boroughs have steadily gained in effective power.[15]

In Greater Stockholm the regional coordination of housing and planning, followed by the complete integration of transportation, led more naturally to a metro plan. The Greater Stockholm Traffic Association, the last and strongest of a series of coordinating bodies, took on regional planning and water and sewer planning on an interim basis in 1968. The final structural reform (1971) created a directly elected Greater Stockholm County Council responsible for regional planning, transportation, health, water supplies and main sewerage; the city and suburban communes kept local planning and housing, for which cooperative arrangements were continued. The new county was based territorially on the old county, which under Swedish law had limited functions, mainly in health. Thus the Stockholm reform preserved continuity with the existing local government system and emerged spontaneously with the support and advice but not dictation of central government. Unlike the city of Toronto and London County Council, the city of Stockholm vigorously promoted the final scheme and voluntarily handed over its public transport system, health services, and many other powers—together with 17,000 of its 48,000 employers—to the new county council. The ground was well prepared and the auguries auspicious.[16]

In each case arguments for more comprehensive urban planning featured strongly in the movement for reform. What has such planning meant in practice, and how has it worked? To tackle this question, we will consider first the planning function itself and then transportation, housing, and financial equalization. Illustrations will be drawn mainly from London and Toronto, because the Stockholm scheme is newer and many of the functional problems had already been solved by the time of its inception.

1. *The Planning Function.* This was largely but not wholly conceived as a broader form of traditional physical planning. In Toronto the function was first assigned to a semiindependent Metropolitan Planning Board including representatives of the municipalities as well as Metro and also appointed laymen; but in 1974 it moved to a committee of the metro council aided by a citizens' advisory group. In London ideas were rather more ambitious. From the start physical planning was closely linked with transportation; the two departments were coordinated by the same committee of the GLC, and subsequently they were formally merged. At the same time, a research and intelligence unit was created in the office of the director general (the chief executive), which later went for a time to the planning department and then returned. A system of corporate planning was established in the same office. The intelligence unit played an important part in some exercises such as the strategic housing plan of 1974. Thus there were efforts in London to arrive at a new conception of "strategic planning," but the elements did not fit together very well. There were gaps between corporate and physical planning, and also, despite administrative coordination, between physical planning and transportation and between planning and housing.

These organizational issues have to be understood against a background of urban change and functional conflicts. Both Metro Toronto and the GLC had to define and develop their distinctive roles, which both saw to some extent in terms of large public works and development projects. Metro Toronto's population grew rapidly from 1.1 million (1953) to 2.1 million (1970) and an estimated 2.8 million (1980). Initially Metro was busy with the provision of new infrastructure—water, main drainage, expressways, a subway system, and new parks—and this works program established its local imprint and reputation.

Zoning laws and development control were responsibilities of the boroughs, and Metro's formal role was only to advise the provincial review bodies (the Ontario Municipal Board for zoning and the Ministry of Housing for subdivisions) about the wisdom of local proposals; but in practice Metro could influence local development decisions fairly effectively during the early period, because of its own works program and the shortage of skilled staff in the rapidly growing suburbs. But as the Metro area became increasingly developed, it became clear that "strategic planning" would need to concentrate more upon sensitive issues of urban renewal and social policy and that Metro's powers and capacities for leadership here were weaker.[17]

Unlike the Toronto planners the GLC started with little scope for urban growth, especially as the council quickly decided to preserve its small part of the metropolitan greenbelt. Nonetheless it started out with highly ambitious plans and projects. One aim was to create a comprehensive road system including four major orbital roads or ringways, three mainly within the GLC area and one beyond it. Subsequently a new subway line was initiated to serve the declining East End. Following the LCC tradition, overspill housing and town development projects were continued beyond the GLC borders, and one major site was found and developed as a "town-in-town" (Thamesmead). Large projects of urban renewal within the central area were initiated, the best known being Covent Garden, which involved the resiting of London's central fruit and vegetable market.

These projects largely fell by the wayside. One reason was a rapid and unforeseen fall in the GLC's population from 8 million when it took office to only about 6½ million in 1980, a decline that was accompanied in the 1970s by the general contraction of public investment funds. But in addition the GLC's planning role had not been thought through and became sadly confused with the parallel and overlapping powers of the London boroughs. Who, for example, was to be responsible for major redevelopment and renewal projects? Both the GLC and the boroughs had the relevant formal powers, the theory being that the former should handle the more "strategic" problems. On this theory the GLC could have concerned itself with large zones of physical blight or substandard housing, with major transportation nodes, with the cultural facilities of central London, or with all such zones and others; but in practice the GLC failed to make good any of these roles and discovered that it was politically easiest to intervene where more than one borough was concerned so that it could play the role of coordinator (as for Covent Garden and Docklands). Again GLC shared development control powers with boroughs in a complicated way, dealing supposedly with proposals of "strategic" significance, but the central area of London—theoretically a key area for such strategic control—was governed by strong boroughs like Westminster and the City that were not prepared to be masterminded.[18]

In theory the answer to such problems lay in the official metro plan which, it was hoped, would establish basic policies for future change and development. Considerable staff time was given to preparing official plans in London and Toronto, and their political importance was often stressed, yet their history in both cases has been one of ineffectiveness and frustration if not futility. In Toronto a draft metro plan was published in 1959, and a final plan was unofficially adopted by the council in 1966, but twelve years later the second royal commission to investigate Metro was deploring the continued absence of an official plan. The Greater London Development Plan (GLDP) appeared in 1969, was the subject of a marathon public inquiry conducted by an expert panel appointed by the minister, and received formal approval from a different minister in 1976, only on a much revised basis, by which time the GLC under changed political leadership had anyhow abandoned many of the plan's proposals.

Metro planning encounters the political problem of winning the support, or overcoming the opposition, of the second-tier authorities. This problem explains the long delays in Toronto, and the fact that the London plan lays down no more than loose indicative targets on matters important to the boroughs such as population, housing densities, office and industrial floor space, and so forth. It eschews any "structural" view of London—for example, whether and where there should be major subcenters. The plan is specific only for some GLC functions (especially roads). Moreover, differences between the plans of the metro authority and the boroughs had to be centrally arbitrated, as in Toronto, and this process proved slow and uncertain.[19]

In optimistic terms, metro planning might be called a learning process. Thus the GLDP was extensively discussed and revised by the GLC during the inquiry itself, as well as after it by ministers. But there was great political and professional uncertainty. There was an attempt to go beyond traditional land use concepts and to base the plan upon economic and social objectives, although the necessary base studies had not actually been done even to the extent that they were for the New York region where, paradoxically, there seems little prospect of strategic planning.[20] This failure over the base studies was partly due to the conception of the GLC Intelligence Unit as primarily a collector of statistics.

In London the conditions for effective planning were anyhow adverse. There was both political and professional uncertainty within the GLC as to whether the traditional dispersal policies for London should be changed, and the central government was more disposed to intervene further in urban affairs than to hand over those basic powers—for example, the controls over industrial and office location—which logically should form part of strategic planning. For example, a succession of government ministers intervened freely over the treatment of London's largest problem area, Docklands, which was being made derelict by the movement of the port downriver. Docklands was the scene of a central-local government partnership scheme, and just when the GLC and the boroughs had agreed upon a program a new minister in 1980 appointed an urban development corporation to rehabilitate Docklands which contained local government representatives but which would operate independently.

In Greater Stockholm metro planning started off more smoothly. A new regional plan was soon prepared and approved by the county council in 1973 and the government in 1974 as the first of a five-year planning cycle. It stressed the conservation of natural resources, proposed research into the implications of energy conservation for urban structure, and signaled a drastic reduction in the volume of big housing projects in favor of more single-family dwellings and more private development.

These policies largely reflected a general policy switch within Sweden. The city's massive development program had enormously improved the supply of housing, but its monumental projects were increasingly critized as a habitat for family life despite their good equipment and facilities. Ecological and environmental values had become much more potent. Within the city an antigrowth party won 11 percent of the vote in 1970, the redevelopment of old parts of the city virtually ceased, compulsory rehabilitation of old housing began under the terms of national legislation, road building was drastically pruned, parking was tightly controlled, and more priority was given to pedestrians and cyclists. Local government financial resources, freely devoted to new development in the 1950s and 1960s, were also at last seriously strained. By 1978 municipal income tax was absorbing 25 percent of incomes—a figure that would be quite inconceivable in any city dependent on local property tax and remarkable even in Stockholm.[21]

At the same time metro planning for Stockholm seemed appreciably less ambitious and forceful than the city's planning had been. The new county council did not, initially, follow the city's tradition of land acquisition for future development needs or offer selective aid to the weaker communes, although it had the power to do so in both cases.

2. *Transportation Planning.*[22] If metro planning has had as yet any definite success, it is probably in this field. Initially it seemed, as some had feared, that a metro scheme would serve primarily to help the road lobby through its incorporation of large numbers of suburban motorists favoring easier mobility and better road access to the city center. Metros also sought to prove themselves by big public works. Toronto's metropolitan expressways and GLC plans for orbital motorways conformed with these initial expectations, but road plans encountered increasing opposition as they impinged upon inner urban areas. In Toronto Metro was compelled in 1971 to halt the Spadina expressway, which it was driving toward the city center, through appeals by its opponents first to the Ontario Municipal Board and then to the provincial cabinet. Later

(1974) Metro canceled its Scarboro expressway. The GLC's motorway box, which would have demolished nearly 10,000 dwellings and cut a swathe through the dense communities of inner London, was bitterly opposed at the public inquiry into the London plan by affected boroughs and by community groups.[23] As a result the Labour party, which won the GLC 1971 election, reversed its earlier position and canceled most of the motorway box proposals.

All three of these metro authorities (London, Toronto, and Stockholm) own and control large efficient public transport systems. Toronto has a new subway system largely built by Metro, the GLC took over the enormous London Transport undertaking in 1970, and Stockholm owns a large and efficient system of rapid transit and buses, although in each case the transport agency operates with some independence from the metro council. These widening responsibilities, combined with a steady swing in public opinion, have led all these metros to become pioneers of a "balanced" transportation policy, despite the initial bias to road developments. In Toronto there has been careful attention to bus and subway interchanges and to park-and-ride schemes, and for its size Toronto has the largest and probably the most efficient public transport system in North America. In Michael Thomson's account of great cities and their traffic, London stands out as the city which has tried hardest for traffic restraint, through a tight system of parking controls, environmental traffic management, reserved bus lanes, and other devices.[24] Greater Stockholm has also done well with public transport coordination.

Nonetheless these metros are still considerably controlled by central governments. The main explanation is financial, because transportation in each area depends heavily and increasingly upon central or provincial subsidies. Developments have hinged upon elaborate transportation studies sponsored jointly by central and metro governments, usually followed by large financial grants based upon a coordinated plan. The Swedish government underwrote 95 percent of the costs of new subway construction as its contribution to the metro plan, while the province of Ontario agreed to contribute 75 percent of capital costs and 25 percent of operating deficits on Toronto's public transport. In Greater London, and increasingly elsewhere, government grants have been integrated so that metro can decide (in theory) the balance between public and private modes, but in practice the choice is not so free because most large decisions must be made jointly and are influenced by financial bargaining.

For example, national trunk roads and major metropolitan roads fulfill rather similar purposes within a big urban area and raise similar problems in their impact upon public transport and the environment. But legal and financial differences remain significant—for example, central governments pay 100 percent for national roads but for metropolitan ones only 50 percent in Toronto and 75 percent in London. In London it was originally intended that the GLC should be responsible for all major highways, but instead some new roads have been shifted into the national category just to help the GLC's finances—although conversely the Department of Transportation prefers the GLC to cope with environmental opposition to road building. Again, the suburban systems of national railways are outside metro control, although there may be arrangements (as there are in Stockholm) whereby Metro buys on contract the suburban rail services it wants, while in Toronto a consortium (the GO system) runs the longer-distance services. Also broader frames of coordination may be needed than metro can provide, for example, a provincial-local government committee coordinates transport in the wider Toronto region.

The financial dependence of metros upon central government naturally restricts their freedom of choice. When central government refused to help finance a costly new subway through Docklands, the GLC decided to go it alone; yet it is unlikely that the line will be built. Joint central-metro planning of big projects is normal and probably inevitable.

More serious is the impact that financial considerations of who pays have on comprehensive planning. Attention to questions of physical and environmental planning are obscured by the question of whether a central government will provide a major new highway free of charge or whether a metro authority must pay much of the cost itself. Coordination between physical and transportation planning is very difficult in any event. It is not made easier by the need to coordinate decisions closely at both central and metro government levels.

The impact of transportation factors upon physical plans has been considerable, but the converse influence of general urban goals upon transportation policies has been less. Administrative integration, which was vigorously pursued in London, seemed to founder upon differences of professional techniques and upon the bias of metro powers and politics toward transportation objectives. The elaborate transportation studies promoted this result, because their normal technique was to predict the location of activities and likely number of trips without considering how far cities could or should be planned to favor some types of movement over others. Thus the London motorway rings were designed for a freefloating pattern of trips without any reference to the desirability of facilitating combined access (by both private and public transport) to suitable subcenters. Nonetheless metro planning offers more scope for coordinating these policies than do other urban systems.[25]

3. *Housing Coordination.* The wide variations of housing conditions in big urban areas are well known. The GLC's estimate of housing shortages in 1966, as measured against an ideal matching of potential households with separate dwellings, ranged from 8 percent in Harrow (an outer borough) to 53 percent in Islington. Residential densities ranged from 7.7 persons per acre (Bromley) to 71.4 (Kensington and Chelsea). In the city of Stockholm there were, thanks to the large public programs, 100,000 more dwellings available in 1970 than twenty years earlier for the same total population, but severe housing stress continued in the older parts. The London and Stockholm data also show the concentration of housing stress among the poorest groups and migrants, even in cities with very large public housing programs. Toronto has comparable problems but much less public housing.

Each metro wanted to increase the supply of low- and moderate-income housing and to locate more such housing within the outer and leafier suburbs, but the means and opportunities for doing so have differed. The GLC had the apparent advantage of inheriting the LCC's enormous stock of public housing and its general powers to build houses within and beyond its area. But political and organizational conditions had changed. The GLC's party political alternations did not allow it to develop the single-minded housing aims of the LCC, while organizationally it proved harder for the GLC to win the cooperation of the outer boroughs than it had been for the LCC to build big estates beyond its borders.

Finding few big sites in outer London where the GLC could itself build, the Labour leadership turned, somewhat reluctantly, to a policy of persuading the outer London boroughs to build and allocate some housing (with GLC assistance) for inner London residents nominated by the GLC. The outer boroughs were reluctant to cooperate, especially but not exclusively those Conservative ones such as Bromley, which hoped that the policy would be revised through a Conservative victory at the next GLC election. Bromley's resistance in fact became a symbol of party conflict. The more usual borough tactics were to offer only small and conditional deals, which yielded 2,548 dwelling (1966–1969)—only about 3½ percent of all public housing built within the capital at that time. These efforts at cooperation continued more weakly under the Conservatives and more forcefully under Labour, but with very limited effects.[26] By 1980 a Conservative GLC was moving to curtail its housing role drastically, with respect to both direct provision and cooperative action, and the housing stock was being handed over to the boroughs.

Metro Toronto's role in housing policy has been surprisingly limited. When Metro started, the city of Toronto had only just built the first municipal project. Metro was given housing powers and developed in the face of local opposition one suburban project (Lawrence Heights) for poorer families from the city of Toronto. Subsequently Metro continued to provide assisted housing for senior citizens, but general-purpose public housing was turned over in 1964 to a new provincial agency, the Ontario Housing Corporation. This corporation built a number of high-rise projects in the suburbs, but their local unpopularity and criticism of their high densities influenced a decline of the program, which nonetheless accounted for most of the 38,650 units of public housing (8.9 percent of all construction) built between 1952 and 1974 in the Metro area, a figure which is high by North American although low by European standards.

Housing policy in Canada, as in the United States, is now to provide assisted rental housing for a wider range of incomes and to spread such housing instead of concentrating it in big, low-income projects. Both Toronto city and Metro have set up nonprofit companies for this purpose. The difficulty is to find enough suitable suburban sites to meet the needs of the central city and to distribute the suburban housing allocations fairly. Theoretically this responsibility has been Metro's all along, but its influence was very shadowy when the Ontario Housing Corporation was building. The linkage of housing with both Metro's physical planning and welfare responsibilities make Metro the obvious authority to plan and where necessary to provide housing, and the last royal commission (1977) proposed that Metro should set housing targets and quotas and also take over the stock of the Ontario Housing Corporation, but the suggested (and very difficult) way of bringing an obstructive borough to heel would be through the still-to-be-approved metro plan, which could then be the basis for an objection before the Ontario Municipal Board regarding housing omissions in the local plan. These tasks could only be achieved if Metro were much more ready to face conflicts with the boroughs and could be sure of provincial support.

Thus neither metro authority seems to have been very successful as a housing coordinator. The strength of suburban pressures and prejudices against public or low-income housing makes the role of coordinator difficult anyway and almost impossible when the coordinating authority shares the prejudices. In Toronto Metro was relieved of its political problems over housing by provincial action, but the action did not solve the problem. In London the political issue was tackled directly but ineffectively. In Stockholm cooperative action between city and suburban communes was gradually built up in advance of the metro scheme. Some quite similar difficulties had to be faced, although the fact that many outer suburbs were working-class and left-wing meant that (as with some town development projects negotiated by the LCC) local interests often welcomed the economic growth which could come from cooperation with a big city. Moreover, central government's arbitral role was crucial in Sweden, especially over requiring a common housing exchange and allocation system to be established between all local governments in the area. This proposal has been frequently made for London but has never been enforced. These examples make it doubtful how far a metro scheme is capable of achieving improvements in housing policy.

4. *Finance.* In Toronto Metro has played a flexible equalizing role. Initially the city was relatively rich and the suburbs poor, but the relationship became reversed as city population fell and urban problems grew, such as a high volume of welfare cases (60 percent of the metro total) and overcrowding among immigrants. Metro first took over almost complete responsibility for education costs while leaving actual administration in the hands of city and boroughs. This helped some suburban boroughs at their time of greatest need but became less necessary as population stabilized. In 1967 it was the city's turn to benefit when Metro took over direct responsibility for short-term welfare payments to individuals in need and for welfare services to old people and others, supplemented by contributions to the many voluntary social organizations in Toronto. Whereas the educational arrangement could encourage local extravagance, the welfare arrangement avoided this danger, although it largely ended local administration. In addition, Metro handles all borrowing by local governments, which reduces the average interest payable as its credit has been good.

The GLC does not have Toronto's scope for financial equalization. The London equalization scheme is very limited and rather curious in its effects, but it is combined with a much broader equalization scheme operated in London (as elsewhere) by central government. In some respect these arrangements work reasonably; for example, education expenditure per head is higher in the inner London area than in any but one of the outer boroughs, which reverses the usual American situation. Inner boroughs naturally spend much more than the outer ones on personal welfare services and housing but with considerable variations due as much or more to policy differences as to variations of need. Equalization does not shield a big-spending borough such as Camden from high rates. The equalizing role which the GLC might be able to play is that of coordinating investment and of making discretionary grants to boroughs and to voluntary bodies to advance social policies.[27]

This comparative review of the three schemes has only skimmed the surface of a big subject. Moreover, each scheme is unique, and these three have had a variable degree of success or effectiveness. But possibly the reasons for these variations are informative about metro government.

1. The schemes varied historically in how far metro evolved cooperatively or was imposed. Stockholm represented continuous evolution, London a clean break. Toronto falls in between, but local government conflict was reduced by the device of indirect election—although the result was a less politically independent or visible metro.

An evolutionary history is no guarantee that a metro scheme will work well, since a fresh start may be necessary to establish a desirable pattern of authorities and powers; but the more novel the system, the more time is needed for metro to establish an effective institutional base. The swift party political alternations in Greater London impeded the creation of a viable institutional role for the GLC. In fact by 1978 the Conservative leadership on the GLC was moving, quite exceptionally in the annals of organizational behavior, to reduce drastically the metro's powers even while still casting around for an alternative "strategic" role. In Toronto the political acceptability of metro was bought at a price of some uncertainty about its powers and permanence, especially its relation to the central city. In Stockholm, the political consensus over the metro scheme was exceptionally high, although it does not follow that the roles of county and city were finally settled.

2. The three schemes varied greatly with respect to the size and character of the area covered. Greater London was (and still is) much the largest in population, but its boundaries were narrowly drawn (because of suburban opposition its area was cut to 616 square miles from the 756 orginally proposed). By contrast with London, Toronto and Stockholm are smaller but rapidly growing and very prosperous cities. Metro Toronto covers only 240 square miles, but for a time it had ample scope for growth. On the other hand Stockholm County with 2,600 square miles has an area large enough to comprehend urban developments for at least a century.

It seems to be much easier for a metro to oversee or to mastermind the growth of a great urban area than for it to cope with the problems of change and decline in the urban core. Growth as embodied physically in the construction of great public works is itself an embodiment and symbol of organizational success. Large urban renewal schemes may also be needed, but these are much more costly and difficult to implement than are developments on the urban frontier. Equally within the urban core local politics is more intensive, interests are thicker on the ground, and the policy issues seem to be intrinsically tougher. Moreover urban growth, although initially costly, will eventually bring in revenue essential for offsetting the costs of urban decline. The management of urban growth can also help solve such functional needs of the city as water supplies, recreational facilities, and sites for low-cost housing.

From the outset Greater London could not control or significantly influence the rapid growth occurring beyond its borders, which was handled through regional plans initiated by central government. Metro Toronto was initially given planning jurisdiction over its surrounding area (a total of 720 square miles), but this was canceled when in the early 1970s the provincial government created adjacent regional municipalities (Peel, York, Durham) possessing many similar powers. As with London, the initiative for planning urban growth is passing to a higher level (the provincial government acting cooperatively with the regional municipalities). Stockholm County, however, is well designed for regional planning. There are also rather different possible ways in which the metro can deal with the urban core in the three cases. In Toronto and Stockholm the existence of large central cities much restricts the metro's role. In London the great scale of old development, and the smaller and more uniform size of the London boroughs when compared with central cities, gives the GLC a much stronger potential role in the urban core. Its difficulties over housing, redevelopment, and so forth have to be understood in this context. One might summarize by saying that Toronto and Stockholm metro governments are primarily designed to deal with urban growth, indeed were called into existence because of the pace of growth, but the former can no longer play this role; whereas Greater London was designed (in fact if not intention) to deal with much larger and very intractable issues of urban renewal and decline.

   3. Metro government becomes harder to operate whenever the powers of the two levels of government are closely intertwined unless the service in question can be treated as highly technical (for example, the relation of local refuse collection to centralized refuse disposal). Functions such as town planning, housing, urban redevelopment, and transportation are not technical in this sense but arouse social conflicts and political passions. The greater the public powers available, the greater are these difficulties of coordination. A complicated metro scheme can only hope to work if there is an efficient way of resolving disputes—either through vesting final authority in the metro government or through prompt arbitration by the central government. Once again London faced the greatest difficulties on this score, and Stockholm the least, with Toronto intermediate. Still, London's greater problems arose in the context of the stronger powers for planning, housing, and redevelopment wielded by the GLC within the urban core as compared with the other two cases.

Metros and Local Government Reform

   These pioneering metro schemes represent the vanguard of more general movements of local government reform which have occurred in

Britain, France, Canada, the United States, and elsewhere. This section will give an overview of the significance of these developments for urban planning.

One possible starting point is the desirable size of new local government units. For some reformers the answer is given by the concept of the city or urban region discussed briefly in chapter 1.[28] As a local government unit the city region would cover the zones of potential growth and development and would be broad enough to enable the processes of urbanization to be steered and guided. It would thereby provide a logical basis for the provision of transportation and other infrastructure, the location of new development, water supplies, environmental conservation, and measures for the equitable allocation of housing, social facilities, and financial resources. While (as noted in chapter 1) boundaries are flexible for these purposes, since much depends upon the pace and scale of urban growth and upon the ambitions of urban planning, clearly a much larger area must be encompassed than that already urbanized. The metro schemes already discussed have illustrated this general argument.

The city region can therefore be advanced not only as a basis for special institutions but for local government reform generally. As such it encounters some general difficulties.

1. Some city regions are much vaster than others—for example, those of the European capital cities. There will therefore be substantial variations in the size of the new local governments, some of which will be enormous and populous regions. Either this result must be accepted, or the zone of the biggest city must be circumscribed, for example, by the recognition of separate subregions. This latter approach would accord with national policy for limiting the magnetism and growth of the biggest urban center (see chapter 4).

2. Some city regions are so closely adjacent or overlapping that it becomes a question of judgment—and also of planning policies—as to whether they should be treated as one or more units.

3. Many areas are still rural and remote from major centers. Yet these more rural areas might possibly be incorporated within a city region framework, since they look to some center for specialized services and would retain a more local form of government as well. Alternatively the city regional reform could be selective and could exclude the remoter rural areas.

These geographic difficulties in the concept of the city region do not destroy its rationale or appeal. The more basic problems are the historical and political objections to destroying existing units such as counties and the absence of political consciousness. These difficulties are likely to become greater as the area to be encompassed becomes wider, since a sharper break with traditions, and also with assumptions about the nature of *local* government, is necessary. Moreover, a city region should include areas which are still largely rural and which may fear urban domination even though they would retain (as with metro schemes) more localized units as well.

The city region concept has had more influence upon local government reform in Britain than anywhere else. The stress on postwar reconstruction and the development of a close-knit system of physical planning forced certain issues into the open. By 1960 it was clear that the plans of cities and of their surrounding counties were weakly coordinated and sometimes contradictory. The expansionist claims of cities, and the difficulty of finding large sites for overspill housing, underlined this problem. Increasingly it was argued that effective plan making must correspond with the desirable limits of future urban expansion and must integrate the interests of city, suburbs, and surrounding countryside. In the 1960s the Ministry of Housing and Local Government (MHLG), the central body for physical planning, proposed a new system of structure and local plans, with the former laying down general principles of development and the latter comprising detailed regulations and proposals for action.[29] The structure plan concept, however, required more rational local government units. The ministry also initiated advisory plans for some city regions.

In addition the close-knit geography of Britain is favorable to the city region concept. In most countries the administrative or economic regions designated by central government are larger (sometimes much larger) than definitions of an urban region, but in some parts of Britain there is or could be a fair correspondence between the two purposes. Much of Britain, but by no means all of it, can be partitioned plausibly into large urban regions. Here, then, to a point, was an integrating blueprint for local government reform.

In the 1960s the MHLG became favorable to the city region concept. A reforming minister, Richard Crossman, set up a Royal Commission on Local Government with this possibility foremost in mind. The commission accepted the doctrine's relevance to three provincial conurbations, for which it advocated an extended type of metro scheme. The commission's main principle, however, was the desirability of "unitary" authorities large enough to combine under one roof all or almost all local government services. Its plans for most of the country followed the uniform population criteria considered necessary for the unitary approach, and they generally respected existing county lines to make the plan more acceptable. Functional and historical criteria thus acquired more significance than the new geography. Nevertheless, one commission member, Derek Senior, produced an eloquent minority

report arguing for dividing England and Wales into thirty-five city regions, each regional authority (with two exceptions) also containing
smaller local governments.[30]

The subsequent local government reform, legislated by a Conservative government in 1972, followed neither of these reports but instead
amalgamated and amended the traditional counties and gave to county
councils for the first time the same jurisdiction over large cities as over
other districts of the county. Still, this act did preserve the commission's
proposal of metro schemes for the large provincial conurbations, extended this concept to six areas, but restricted closely the boundaries of
these new metropolitan counties. The city region concept transmuted
into a much more limited metro concept, and the traditional distinction
between big cities and relatively rural counties was recreated on a
broader scale. The concept of the structure plan which had also been
implemented had to be applied to local government areas that usually
bore little resemblance to the original notion of a city region.

These provincial conurbations had no previous tradition of an overall
authority like the London County Council, and the new metro counties
were given weaker powers than the GLC. Functions such as urban
renewal, housing, local planning, and development control seem likely
to be handled almost exclusively by the district councils, thus reducing
the London type of conflict. The metro county can exercise influence
through the medium of its structure plan, but apart from its strong direct
stake in transportation, it will have to rely largely upon persuasion to
arrange implementation of the plan. Its reserve powers of intervention
are weak, and a basic conflict between county and local planning can
only be resolved through the awkward process of ministerial arbitration.
Moreover the strategic capacity of a metro county to steer development
is also limited by the earlier transfer of water and drainage functions
from local governments to centrally appointed regional boards. Because of restricted boundaries, most or all metro counties seem likely to
have falling populations. Just like London and now Toronto, they will be
unable to balance growth against decline, and their intervention in the
micropolitics of the inner city will be, as history already shows, a delicate
and difficult matter.[31]

Inspired by another royal commission, a more radical Scottish reform
introduced the concept of five large regional authorities together covering the entire country. Two of these regions, Strathclyde and Lothian,
correspond to two big city regions based upon the cities of Glasgow
and Edinburgh. Strathclyde has 2.5 million people (almost half Scotland's population) and covers 3,200 square miles, including many remote places. It contains only eleven districts, and both district and
regional councils are directly elected, but regions have the strongest

functions. The reform has been criticized for creating unnecessarily large and remote districts, but it does embody the city region idea much more fully than the English reform.[32]

The city region concept has had some influence in other countries. For example, in the Netherlands there have been proposals for replacing the traditional pattern of provincial governments with different, sometimes smaller governments that would have a city regional basis in a number of cases. The new authorities might also differ in structure and functions from the historic provinces and might embody a new role of strategic planning and management in relation to smaller local governments. There already exists the elected Rijnmond regional council, covering Rotterdam and twenty-two other local governments on both banks of the Rhine estuary; it is primarily concerned with strategic planning rather than execution.[33]

In France the great number and small size of the local communes pose obvious problems for urban planning. Despite laws encouraging mergers, there existed in 1975 more than 36,000 communes—much the same as in 1851—of which more than half had under 500 inhabitants and only thirty-nine had more than 100,000. The communes include substantial cities like Lyons and Bordeaux, but the growing urban regions of France all include a large number of small units. This problem has been tackled through the creation of indirectly elected syndicates of communes, each district thus formed being responsible for a group of functions which could be augmented by agreement. The creation of such districts required strong majority support among the affected communes or else the initiative of the prefect supported by at least half the communes.

Under a 1966 law, however, a type of metro authority was compulsorily introduced for the four agglomerations of Bordeaux, Lille, Lyons, and Strasbourg. The council of each of these "urban communities" is directly elected, and its powers are considerable, including urbanization plans, main highways and public transport, secondary and further education, and so forth. The many existing communes persist at the local level. The same system has been adopted by majority vote of the communes concerned in five other conurbations, and altogether over 4 million people live in the nine provincial urban communities.[34]

The one real French example of the city region concept is the creation of the Paris region (see next chapter), but this is not part of local government. The subsequent creation of provincial urban communities owed a good deal to the government's regional policy of checking the growth of Paris. If provincial centers were to counter the attractive powers of the Paris region, they had to be planned and developed effectively.

As urbanization came later in France than in England, problems of transportation, development, and land were still greater. The professional and expert resources for tackling these problems were largely lodged in the agencies, field services, and special "missions" (joint task forces of experts) belonging to central government. Only the largest communes had substantial staffs of their own. Thus the urban community reform was dictated also by the need to simplify the coordination and application of planning by government agencies. In Britain the administrative needs or convenience of central government played some part, but a smaller one, in local government reforms. A major difference is that at all levels political and administrative influence interpenetrate in France, whereas in Britain much clearer lines are drawn between the institutions of central and local government. The political influence of the communes has secured their retention, but their organizational weakness strengthens the role of the urban community.

In Germany the Ruhr conurbation has had since 1920 a unique regional agency responsible for planning, land acquisition, resource conservation, and financial aid to the many local governments within its area. Generally it exercises a planning and coordinative role, but it can undertake developmental tasks—for example, it has participated in the building of a new town. This regional agency has an assembly with 60 percent of members drawn from local government and 40 percent from economic organizations. It is responsible to a minister of the land and represents as much an example of state-local and public-private cooperation as of local government reform as such.[35]

Within the United States there is enormous interest in metro problems and solutions, but there are few truly comprehensive metro schemes to examine. The problems of urban regions are being tackled through two very different kinds of development, however. Because of the variety and complexity of arrangements throughout the fifty states, this brief account will be very simplified.

One approach being taken involves city-county consolidations, or expanding the powers of counties. The county in most American states is traditionally a rather weak and amorphous unit concerned with the local administration of state functions such as justice, highways, welfare, and health services. The late nineteenth-century modernization of English counties did not happen in the United States, although there have been piecemeal reforms in some places. By accidents of history, however, some counties have at least a partial correspondence with a metropolitan area, in which case the county may become the focus for consolidation proposals or may develop an important role as a service provider.

Such a proposal (at its fullest) entails the conversion of the county into a city which then absorbs all the other urban governments within the area. More usually most or even all of the existing governments are left in being and the county-cum-city functions as a top-level type of metro authority. In fact, while many attempts have been made at such reorganizations, they have succeeded in only a few cases. The successes have been mainly in southern states and include Baton Rouge (Louisiana), Nashville–Davidson County (Tennessee), and the best known scheme, Dade County (Florida).

The Dade metro plan has been described as the only successful two-tier experiment in the United States. This is because it attempted a novel and rational distribution of powers between the two levels of government and also allowed metro to lay down standards for the smaller local governments and to take over functions where necessary. Some upward transfers of functions have taken place which caused much conflict, but the scheme survived. Metro has drawn up a general land use plan and water and sewer plans and has organized a bus system. It has acquired independent sources of finance as well. The political conditions for success here seem to have included the presence of many retired people and other recent migrants interested in efficient government and the fact that half the population lived in unincorporated areas depending directly upon the county for services. Still, the scheme in Dade County, like most county reorganization schemes in the United States, does not cover the whole urbanized area.

These few schemes have made a small dent upon American metropolitan problems and have indeed been outweighed by the proliferation of new municipalities. No reform scheme has worked in any of the biggest urban regions. Unlike Canada or Germany, most states in the American federation have taken little initiative in local reform, beyond passing laws stipulating the local majorities needed for reforms to pass. Virginia is one exception, with its arrangements for monitoring change in local government.[36]

Some counties seem to have emerged as important planning authorities and service providers in default of alternatives. For example, Los Angeles County and Cook County (Illinois) find themselves for reasons of geography with a substantial stake in urban planning. The former also provides many services for the unincorporated islands within its territory and variable services on contract for smaller local governments. This flexible but lopsided and unsystematic pattern has some virtues, including perhaps the freedom of local governments to decide whether to provide for themselves or to buy from the county.[37] But counties rarely offer a systematic response to the problems of urban growth.

The other American development is the creation of councils of government (COGs) in metropolitan areas. COGs are assemblies of elected officials drawn from local governments and usually lack executive power. They are not metro governments but weak agencies for overall coordination and planning. Their impact is much limited both by lack of powers and by difficulties of coordination.[38]

First, COGs only exist at all as a rule because the federal government made money available for metropolitan planning. A COG's teeth derive solely from the ability of a federal or state agency to nominate it as the relevant clearinghouse for ensuring that a grant paid to local government accords with the provisions of an areawide plan. The vetting powers of a COG are limited because it is reluctant to offend any of its local governments. For the very same reason any areawide plan produced by a COG is likely to be a flimsy or superficial document. If a COG were directly elected, it would acquire more authority and would develop more interest in planning, and this is the aim of some civic groups, but the support of the state legislature and a local referendum are needed for this purpose. Success is rare, but Oregon enacted a relevant bill for the greater Portland area in 1978.

Second, special agencies are often created at the metropolitan level to plan and operate facilities in such fields as transportation, water resources, air pollution control, and health. Theoretically a COG should have an overall planning role which coordinates these special agencies, and some COGs attempt to do just this. Unfortunately federal and state agencies often prefer to work through these special metropolitan agencies and to ignore the COG. As a planning body, therefore, a COG lacks either the capacity or, usually, the will to exercise much influence over either higher-level agencies or the local governments which comprise it It may to some extent act as a clearinghouse for information and sometimes for the avoidance of duplication over grants-in-aid, but not (as a rule) as a planning agency.

The complexity of metropolitan government in the United States is shown by the problems of Association of Bay Area Governments (ABAG) which covers 9 counties, 93 municipalities, and over 500 special purpose districts centering on San Francisco. In this region there are important special purpose authorities such as the Metropolitan Transit Commission (which controls the new rapid transit provided by Bay Area Rapid Transit, or BART), Bay Area Comprehensive Health Planning Council, Bay Area Air Pollution Control District, the state Coastal Commission, and others appointed in various ways. ABAG has attempted on occasion to take over the duties of some of these agencies, or at least to become the body for certifying grant approvals, but with only occasional success. The cities and counties which comprise ABAG must each vote a majority on each issue. Nonetheless it has attracted some political interest and one day may become directly elected. Meanwhile it has strengthened its professional staff and its links with the state governor's office of planning and research, which also has a problem of coordination.[39]

More impressive, indeed unique, is the metropolitan council for the Twin Cities region of Minnesota. Success here has rested upon the backing of the state legislature and governor. The governor, not local governments, appoints the metropolitan council, though he chooses individuals of local standing from large constituencies. In 1977 a move to make the council elective failed in the state legislature, and it is therefore a chosen instrument of the state and also the clearinghouse for federal agencies concerned with pollution control, health, and transportation. It exercises influence over the regional special agencies and local governments through the device of coordinating policy boards backed by powers to review the plans and budgets of some agencies and to suspend for a year projects of "metropolitan significance." It is also responsible for allocating quotas of moderate- and low-income housing among the suburban governments, and a rich suburb which refused to comply was denied approval of an open space grant. The metropolitan council prepared a plan for the "metropolitan urban service area" and is allowed to alter inconsistent local plans. It has also made considerable contributions toward financial equalization, especially through pooling 40 percent of the growth in nonresidential property values and through the equalization of school costs up to the average state cost per pupil unit. To a point the metropolitan council for the Twin Cities has acted like a genuine strategic planning body, although its ability to influence the regional special agencies is in practice often very limited, especially where it does not appoint any of their members. It is also unique. Most COGs are less effective even than ABAG.[40]

Evaluation of Metro Planning

Theoretically, metro governments are well placed to advance the goals of efficiency and equality advanced in chapter 1. They generally have considerable responsibilities for planning and developing basic infrastructure and for coordinating land uses throughout a metropolitan area. These powers should be conducive to improved efficiency. The equality goal is helped by the broad area which a metro covers and which should help it to distribute the goods and bads of environmental change in a fair manner. Also metros usually have powers to help the poorer local units and to distribute the provision of housing more equitably, as well as sometimes to contribute to the renewal of blighted areas and to their economic and social rehabilitation.

Unfortunately the track record of existing metro governments does not seem to realize this potential very well. There have been some limited successes (for example, in transportation) and some serious failures (for example, in housing provision). We have to look to organizational and political factors in order to understand the failures, and we must also consider the same factors in order to appreciate the kind of planning function which a metro might perform.

Table 1. Populations of Metropolitan and Second-Tier Authorities

Metropolitan authority	Population	Second-Tier authorities	Average population
Greater London	6,660,000	33	200,000
English metro counties (6)	1,950,000[a]	6[a]	320,000
Metro Toronto	2,500,000	6	420,000
Stockholm County	1,500,000	23	65,000
French urban communities (9)	460,000[a]	28[a]	16,500

[a]Average.

The basic organizational problem of metro governments is their position as "pig in the middle" between central (or state) government on the one hand and strong second-tier local governments on the other. Table 1 shows the balance between the metro and the second-tier authorities in a number of cases, indicating the substantial size of the boroughs or districts in London, Toronto, and the English metro counties. The ratio of only six smaller governments to one metro in these cases (except for London) may itself suggest the difficulties of the metro in planning and coordination. Its span of control over the authorities to be coordinated seems to be too narrow and looks narrower still if viewed in a geographic rather than population context. Still, in Stockholm County and much more so in France the average size of the second-tier units is considerably smaller.

The table does not show the large size of the central city, which except in London has continued in existence as a second-tier unit with little or no change in its previous boundaries. It is true that the relative importance of the central city has declined as population moves out—sometimes drastically, as in Toronto's case—but this process gradually ceases unless the metro's boundaries are continuously extended. In the schemes listed the central city still accounts for between about one-quarter and one-half of metro population. It has lost some of its functions to the metro government, but those which it retains are still substantial and usually much greater (in terms of expenditure, for example) than those of metro. If metro is indirectly elected, the city will have a powerful influence within the counsels of metro as well as being an independent political force. In all cases the city tends to be politically more visible.

A further problem of these arrangements, which relates to the earlier discussion of size and structure, is the relative remoteness of *both* levels of local government, especially within the area of the central city. The citizen is represented by two sets of councillors, but each set governs a large unit. The large size of many European councils, in contrast with North American ones, helps the councillor-citizen ratios but does not eliminate the difficulty of multiple but remote representation. Public participation exercises are an inadequate substitute, since they depend upon an effective representative system. Experiments with area management schemes represent another attempt to overcome "remoteness" and generally combine an administrative goal (more effective and coordinated service delivery to a locality) with a political goal (stepping up the role of the ward councillor or providing a forum for complaints and information). The evidence is that such schemes are strongly frustrated by bureaucratic departmentalism and difficulties of delegation, although they sometimes increase contacts between citizens and councillors.[41]

Under these conditions a metro scheme seems likely to work well only if the central or state government genuinely devolves sufficient power to the metro authority and also provides prompt arbitration of disputes between the two levels of local government. Unfortunately these conditions are rarely met. Central governments, whatever their first intention, seem often to treat metros as if they were ordinary local authorities; and only in the case of Stockholm (among those investigated) does arbitration seem to work reasonably well. There is also need for regular review of the powers, resources, and areas of metro authorities. Toronto has a history of frequent reviews, but generally this requirement is poorly met.

It seems difficult for metro governments to build up an independent political base. Indirect election certainly helps cooperation between metro and its constituent local governments, but this cooperation will not extend beyond purposes which can be generally agreed upon. This seems to be the situation in Toronto. In Winnipeg, by contrast, the metro council is directly elected from constituencies deliberately designed to break away from those in use for the second-tier authorities. This is said to have increased the capacity of metro to make independent decisions, but at the cost of considerable conflict with the constituent units.[42]

Direct election, however, will not necessarily establish the political importance and independence of a metro government. In England local government is permeated by the national political parties, and the GLC election in particular has become a test of the popularity of the party holding office nationally, especially when it has occurred at a mid-term point between general elections. On a few occasions, such as the urban motorway controversy in 1970, a London issue has gained real significance, but even then national political issues dominated the actual voting. The lack of agreement between the parties about the GLC's role makes it harder for that authority to attract political interest. In this situation ministers and civil servants feel inclined or impelled to take the initiative in distinctive London issues such as the future of Docklands and to withhold the support for the GLC which is required for its coordinative tasks.

The political interplay between three (and sometimes four) levels of government is variable. In Toronto local councils are small, and elections are nonpartisan and frequent—every two years for Metro, although pressure for a longer term is strong. In Sweden, local councils are large and elections are partisan, but the minority group participates in local administration, terms are long (four years), and national and local elections are synchronized and embody proportional representation. In England, local councils are large, elections are strongly partisan, councillors serve for four years, and local and national elections are normally separated. Inevitably there will be political as well as organizational conflicts between the three levels of government. Of the three schemes considered earlier, London has shown the most volatile and partisan politics in this sense. By contrast, Swedish political conditions have made for a greater degree of consensus politics in Stockholm, although this situation has now changed, while Toronto politics revolve much more around institutional rivalries and specific issues.

Greater London may represent a special case, partly because (as was said earlier) it is a more ambitious scheme than most. But everywhere the political difficulties of building an effective institutional base at the metro level are considerable, inasmuch as both higher level and lower level governments are often more solidly entrenched. A fairly successful scheme like Metro Toronto needs continually to prove its worth, which becomes harder if there is no more growth to manage and if provincial government takes over regional initiatives with respect to planning, transportation, and other matters. Frederick Gardiner, the first and strongest chairman of Metro Toronto, eventually favored creating a single consolidated city—the solution which had originally been rejected as politically impracticable. Metro Toronto is probably secure, but the political rivalries of cities and their suburbs remain entrenched within the convoluted structure of metro schemes.

It is sometimes suggested that a metro government needs to be headed by a powerful leader, such as a strong mayor in American cities, in order to establish a political impact upon the populace. There is force in this contention if the conventions of local government could be changed, but it may also be questioned how far the coordinating and planning tasks of a metro require or make for a strong personality. Frederick Gardiner in Toronto was the strong man who got metro off the ground, but he was appointed by the provincial government. In the United States the Twin Cities regional council owns its relatively strong authority to appointment by the governor. The Ruhr regional agency is responsible to a land minister. These examples raise the question of whether the first requirement for a metro's effectiveness may be not political independence but strong backing from a central or state government.

Metro governments possess a mixture of planning and operating powers, but the former are usually much broader than the latter. In the sphere of transportation the two functions may be quite closely integrated because the metro itself provides major services. In other fields, such as urban renewal and housing, the metro can make plans but depends largely upon other bodies for implementation. This mismatch of powers poses problems. The capacity of a metro as overall planning agency is likely to be weakened by its simultaneous possession of big operational functions which will bend its planning function in their direction. It need not follow that no operating powers at all should exist in metro's repertoire but rather that any such powers should represent selective interventions for furthering its overall planning. On the other hand if metro is to be primarily judged as a direct service provider, then it needs an adequate and balanced range of operating responsibilities.

Transportation and housing are the two functions which, along with urban redevelopment, have raised the strongest political passions about metro policies. In both these cases metro policies have been changed as a result of strong local objections. Metros have faltered over building or sponsoring low-income housing in the suburbs, and they have also drawn back from driving expressways through inner areas. In each case strong objections from the local boroughs or districts were an important factor. But the effects of the policy changes were different. Metro's housing role is strongly related to equalization aims, and if these are blocked its role is weakened or completely negated. Expressway setbacks are much less serious because an alternative policy is practicable ("balanced transportation") and because metro possesses strong direct powers, including the power of driving at least some expressways through in the face of opposition.

These political histories suggest that metros may usually be unable to

pursue assertive or aggressive policies. A big city government possessed a formidable array of direct powers and a strong political clout.
In some European countries a city seemed more able to provide housing for poorer citizens beyond its borders than a metro can within its own
area. Part of this difference may be due to changes in national housing
policy, but another reason with respect to both the housing and
transportation issues is metro's much greater exposure to local pressures through the second-tier authorities, especially where these are
large and powerful. A compensating advantage for metro may or
perhaps should be that it can take a broader, more balanced, and less
politically partisan view of issues and developments that affect the
whole urban area. This is the "strategic planning role" hopefully conferred upon metros by many observers, although the role's specification
has always been cloudy. I will consider it in the last chapter.

American experience with metro schemes also confirms these con-
clusions. The method of city-county consolidation has produced a form
of metro government in a few cases, but the county often covers an
inadequate area and the method seems inapplicable to the largest
urban regions. The alternative device of councils of government should
be judged by its potential to establish a new kind of strategic planning
body. The conditions for a successful performance of this role are not
usually met, and improvements almost certainly depend upon stronger
initiatives by state governments (see later).

The arguments for metro schemes which emerged earlier in this
chapter included greater equalization of services and resources, a
logical allocation of functions which would balance local and metropolitan interests, a capacity for overall planning, and a reinterpretation of
local democracy to accord both with the facts of large-scale urban
growth and the renaissance of very localized communities. Metro
schemes have made some if uneven progress toward the first two goals
but have done less well with respect to the aims of planning and
democracy. Metro schemes often seem to be unhappily poised between central and local government where their scale, functions, and
political credibility are concerned.

4: Central Government and Urban Regions

National Urban Policies

The phrase "national urban policy" has variable meanings for people, politicians, and government departments. Since 1945, however, three phases of policy might be roughly distinguished. In the first phase some European governments sought to divert new growth from their largest cities to depressed regions. Next, efforts were made to coordinate economic development and urban policies at the regional level, usually with very limited success. In the third phase, governments became concerned with cities as themselves problem areas, and competition grew over the allocation of government aid. Throughout these developments there is also a common theme—the efforts of central governments, generally in partnership with local governments, to establish improved planning frameworks for the urban region. This development is examined in later sections of this chapter.

Urban Dispersal Policies

The first phase of national policies was inaugurated in Britain by an influential royal commission report in 1940 (the Barlow report).[1] The commission concluded that the rapid growth of London was not only strategically dangerous (a fairly obvious point in 1939, as perhaps again in 1980) but also had strong social and economic disadvantages. Some of these drawbacks came from overcrowding and high densities in the inner areas, which could be considered a problem of structure rather than size, but other drawbacks were long journeys to work, transportation problems, and the alleged "anomie" of suburban life, which could only be intensified by further peripheral growth. Moreover, and this to most observers seemed the crucial point, London was absorbing new industrial growth at the expense of many old industrial areas where unemployment was extremely high. The Barlow solution envisaged the physical containment of the capital and the diversion of further industrial growth through a system of licensing to other parts of Britain. A vigorous minority report also stressed the value of new towns as a means of decongesting the capital and other big cities.

Thus the lines of postwar policy were laid down: on the one hand controls and incentives for steering industries to depressed areas; on the other hand a new form of urban regional planning for the capital, with a stress on population dispersal, greenbelt, and new towns. Both these programs were vigorously followed after the war, but by different agencies following largely unrelated policies. The unified view of the Barlow report was never recaptured, and its minority report proposal—of unifying industrial and physical planning in the hands of a single ministry—was not followed. But the diagnosis and prescriptions have been influential to this day.

The French equivalent to Barlow was a single book written by J. F. Gravier, *Paris et le désert français* (1947). The "desert" in question was not only the economic vacuum created by the location of growth industries around Paris, and the demographic contrast between the size of the capital and other French cities, but the cultural monopoly of Paris in higher education, science, and the arts. By then the government was offering subsidies for the decentralization of industries, although they usually moved no further than other towns in the Paris region. Still, a fuller version of a Barlow policy came with the increasing stress of French economic planning upon regional development—in particular, upon bringing industries to the mainly rural western half of the country and to old industrial areas in the northeast. This led, as in Britain, to controls on industrial location in Paris and to graded incentives for industry to move to various development zones (1954–1955) but not immediately to comprehensive plans for the Paris region or provincial cities.[2]

In smaller European countries similar policies developed. The Netherlands is remarkable for the comprehensive nature of its physical planning, influenced by its small land area and history of essential land reclamation from the North Sea. Its central agglomeration, the Randstadt ("rim city"), contains a string of major towns (Amsterdam, The Hague, Rotterdam, and others) and holds about a third of the national population. From 1956 onward the National Physical Planning Office worked to control the growth of the Randstadt through its influence upon provincial and municipal plans, while economic incentives were used to stimulate various growth points in the mainly rural areas of the north and east. In Sweden by 1970 the whole of the northern half of the country was eligible for industrial and investment subsidies, designed to offset the pull exercised by Stockholm and a few other cities upon new industrial growth. Within Sweden's small population and large area, Stockholm is a dominant center (containing 18 percent of the population in 1970), but it is not big enough to present the intrinsic growth problems of some capitals. The Netherlands and Sweden have moved cautiously in imposing location controls upon private firms, but they have actively promoted the dispersal of government offices from the capital—as have Britain and France. Other European countries (for example, Denmark and Greece) have pursued their versions of a Barlow policy.[3]

It is worth noting that even more rigorous policies of containment have been applied to capital cities in communist countries. In Poland "threshold theory" was used as a justification for trying to keep Warsaw's population below 1 million, since above that level a big investment in public transport was said to be essential; but another factor has been claims of balanced geographic growth. Moscow has been kept much the smallest of all big capital cities in relation to national population—a mere 4.4 percent in 1970. The city's growth has been steered into a circle of new towns, and total urban size controlled in the interest of vigorous regional development programs elsewhere in the USSR.[4]

In the United States the long-standing contrast between vast, sprawling cities and declining or stagnant rural areas and small towns has often attracted critical comment. But while the Departments of Agriculture and Commerce have developed aid programs for declining areas, these have never been connected with the control of urban growth. Such control policies would have to contend with the well-entrenched rights of industrialists and landowners and with the ideological assumption that urban growth is a product of individual free choice—although the results are often morally deplored. The race riots of the 1960s stimulated concern about the effects of unstructured migration into the big cities. President Nixon struck a familiar American note when he contrasted the inefficiency and ungovernability of big cities with the traditional virtues of small towns:

> The American national government has responded to urban concerns in a haphazard, fragmented, and often woefully short-sighted manner (as when the great agricultural migrations from the rural South were allowed to take place with no adjustment or relocation arrangements whatever). What we never had is a policy. . . .[5]

Perhaps the nearest equivalent to an American Barlow was the 1972 report of the Commission on Population Growth and the American Future. Alarmed by the prospect of the emergence by the year 2000 of twenty-five gigantic consolidated urban regions, the commission urged

federal encouragement for growth centers in declining regions as well
as middle-sized metropolitan areas of as many as 500,000 people so as
to reduce the spread of megalopolis. Its report was vague about means,
however, and as with many other American reports relied upon more
research and presidential leadership.[6] The latter had been provided for
in 1970 by legislation which requires the president to issue a biannual
report on urban policy. These reports have not yet managed to translate
rhetoric into policy on the issues of population and employment distribution.

Urban Policies and Economic Aid

In the next policy phase collisions occurred between urban policy
goals and regional policies of economic aid, and new planning
frameworks were created. Regional aid policies have largely focused
upon relieving unemployment wherever it occurs, which may be in a big
city, a remote mining village, or the countryside. The long-term aim has
usually been to offset the migration and unemployment or underemploy-
ment caused by a rapid contraction of jobs in agriculture and in heavy or
old industries such as mining, steel, shipbuilding, and cotton textiles.
Although every government started with priority areas, the list of zones
claiming and receiving aid steadily grew everywhere. The relation to
urban policy was uncertain despite increasing use of the "growth point"
concept, which stands for the policy of concentrating, not diffusing, the
government aid available but is indeterminate about the size and other
charactoristics of a growth point. (For example, many new towns promote dispersal from cities, but others promote concentration of previously
scattered facilities in mining areas and elsewhere. The size of growth
points therefore varies widely, their location is affected by political
competition for government aid, and their function relates uneasily to the
established hierarchy of urban places.)[7]

Regional assistance policies and urban policies are nearly always the
responsibility of different government departments having different
aims, policies, and techniques. The former are executed by industrial or
economic departments, the latter by departments concerned with environmental planning, land use and housing, and sometimes also with
local government generally. The organizational frameworks vary sharply. Economic or industrial assistance is funneled from the top downward,
because usually only national governments have the resources to provide aid or to steer industries to different areas, whereas environmental
and land use planning moves to some extent from the bottom upward,
because local governments usually exercise the powers and have a
degree of autonomy. This division of policies and interests occurs

almost everywhere, whether or not a Barlow-type policy is being followed, and produces many conflicts and difficulties of coordination.[8]
Theoretically, regional organizations (or sometimes the states in federal
systems) provide an integrating framework. They provide the focus
where interregional and intraregional policies overlap and should be
reconciled.[9] In practice the regional system, whatever it is, cannot easily
sustain this load or meet this challenge.

In England and Wales after 1945 there was a parallel but unrelated
development of the two policies. A new Ministry of Town and Country
Planning, acting in partnership with joint committees of local governments, encouraged the preparation of outline advisory plans for several
large urban regions such as Greater London, the west Midlands, and
the northeast coast, and the Scottish Office did the same for Clydeside.
Although technically unsophisticated, prepared on a shoestring, and
purely advisory in nature, several such plans were influential. They were
so because of postwar enthusiasm for physical reconstruction, the
temporary freezing of land values, and the acceptability at that time of
policies which had featured in the minority Barlow report—urban
decongestion and containment, greenbelts, new towns—and which the
new central ministry worked hard to support. Several plans bore the
imprint of a single consultant, Sir Patrick Abercrombie, who had also
signed the Barlow minority report.

These broad urban plans bore little relationship to the industrial location policies that were being vigorously and simultaneously pursued by
the Board of Trade. These policies brought large numbers of new
factories and jobs to the old industrial areas of northern England, Scotland, and South Wales. Inevitably there were conflicts between the
claims of these development areas and the new towns in the south for
the mobile industries which were being siphoned off from London and
Birmingham in particular. There were also conflicts within the development areas between the policy of decongesting big cities like Liverpool
and Glasgow and of pumping in new jobs to reduce unemployment
there. These conflicts were arbitrated seriatim through interdepartmental committees or bargaining, but they were never really resolved.[10]

In 1964 a new Department of Economic Affairs was set up to prepare
a national economic plan and associated plans for regional development. Eight economic planning regions were recognized for England,
and one each for Wales and Scotland. The existing interdepartmental
machinery at regional level was consolidated and strengthened and
was linked with advisory regional planning councils appointed by the
minister and drawn in equal parts from local government, industry, and
independent experts or personalities. The quick collapse of the national
plan left these regional councils with few guidelines for preparing their

plans, but they nevertheless produced a large number of not very influential regional studies, strategies, and other documents. With the abolition of the department itself in 1969, this regional machinery was transferred to the new Department of the Environment, where it became more closely associated with physical planning. Industrial development and control policies continued to reside with the Department of Industry, which built up its own regional machinery. In 1979 the regional councils (but not the regional planning boards of civil servants) were abolished.

What difference did this experiment make to regional planning? In its brief life the Department of Economic Affairs made some attempts to integrate urban and industrial policies, for example, by promoting more new towns as industrial growth points in the less prosperous regions. It established controls over office as well as industrial development in London, and it stimulated a substantial dispersal of government office work from the capital, although with no clear view of desirable destinations. But the policy integration was not strong. The main political effect of the regional councils was to step up the competition for government favors, and for the first time the southern regions had spokesmen who could argue, occasionally with some success, for a relaxation of industrial and office controls. A more enduring effect of the machinery may have been the fostering of a closer partnership at regional level between central and local government. This came about partly through the forums provided by the regional planning councils themselves, but also because their existence stimulated the county councils to join together in "standing conferences" covering the same regions. As a consequence there was some rivalry between the planning councils and the standing conferences, to resolve which a tripartite system of regional planning evolved in some regions, to which the regional council, the standing conference, and government departments all on occasion contributed. The difficulties of joint working had not been resolved everywhere before the abolition of the regional planning councils in 1979. Still, it is possible that an experiment which started with the intention of regionalizing national economic planning will end by doing more to regionalize local planning on a partnership basis.[11]

In France, by contrast, economic planning triumphed over physical planning at the regional level. In the early 1960s the French economic plan was regionalized under the auspices of the General Planning Commission, and a special agency (Délégation á l'Aménagement du Territoire et à l'Action Régionale, or DATAR) was set up in the prime minister's office to expedite policies for decentralization and regional development. In each of twenty-one new regions a regional prefect was appointed who was assisted by a personal staff, a committee of departmental officials, and an advisory council drawn from local government, industry and agriculture, and local experts or notables. The regional plan followed a process of national guidelines, regional consultations and preparation, and central review which synchronized it with resource and investment priorities settled ultimately in Paris, although a share of capital investment was left to regional discretion. National investment funds and credit facilities were allocated through these plans, assisted by the special aid available from DATAR for desirable regional projects.[12] This machinery was partly democratized in 1972 when each region received an assembly comprising the local senators and deputies together with representatives elected by local governments. Each assembly acquired a small independent budget, but resources continued mainly to be distributed from the center, and the regional prefect's control of the planning machinery largely continued.[13]

These developments and the activities of DATAR led to a closer integration of urban and regional goals than was the case in England. The fifth plan (1966–1969) introduced the concept of *métropoles d'équilibres* in the form of eight provincial cities which were to act as countermagnets to the attractions of Paris. Educational and cultural establishments, and some government offices and research units, were moved from the capital to these cities or were set up there. Attempts were made to organize industries into "poles of growth" related to particular centers. Simultaneously study groups were set up (1966) jointly by DATAR and the Ministry of Equipment to prepare plans for the same eight provincial conurbations. A further aspect of the policy was the 1966 law for a compulsory merging of communes into new urban communities. It was thought that the provincial cities would be more effective with unified governments and comprehensive development plans.

The policy faced many difficulties, however. First, the administrative reform of the Paris region, further discussed later, created a powerful new organization with ambitious plans for urban growth. When national growth rates declined, the countermagnet concept became harder to realize. Second, the list of métropoles d'équilibres was deliberately biased toward the periphery of France because of the broad range of Parisian influence and sometimes incorporated two main cities (such as Nantes and St. Nazaire) so as to cope with local rivalries. Third, the policy was open to the objection that some of the chosen cities might themselves become too large and congested and might in their turn suck life from smaller towns, many of which were simultaneously being designated as growth centers for declining agricultural areas. As in Britain, although to a much smaller extent, this objection was sometimes met by local plans for urban dispersal which included, for example, a new town for Lyons and another for Marseilles. This, like other cases of conflicting aims, involved the French planners in a high degree of fine tuning. For example, in 1973 offices moving from Paris to Lyons received relocation subsidies, but industries decentralizing from Lyons also received subsidies and tax benefits. Finally these problems and local political pressures caused less emphasis to be placed upon building up the big provincial cities, and more upon the time-honored virtues of *villes moyennes,* or medium-sized towns.[14]

The greater formal coherence of French policies disguises a continued split between the aims of economic and physical planning. The planning commission wrested the initiative from the Ministry of Housing, which was making twenty-year physical plans for urban and regional development, through its ability to fit regional plans into a medium-term system of resource allocation combined with longer-term perspective studies using economic models. These methods appeared as more "scientific" and economically relevant than the old physical planning, which resembled that of Abercrombie. Still, the Ministry of Equipment (later called Environment), which was formed in 1966 by a merger of the Ministries of Housing and Public Works, created a strong new department for housing, urban planning, and civil engineering. This ministry is closely involved in the preparation (with the urban communities) of urban development master plans. Theoretically these master plans are linked with regional planning through their vetting by an interministerial committee and the preparation of a public investment plan for each conurbation. But the linkages do not seem close or effective except for the Paris region, which corresponds (as the other regions do not) to a distinctive city region. French planning has been more successful in the economic than the urban sphere, and the two activities are to some extent in conflict.[15]

In the United States federal legislation was passed in 1962 to aid depressed areas designated by the Department of Commerce. Direct industrial incentives or controls were not used, and financial assistance was given for public works, principally roads. The department was unable to resist congressional pressure for extending eligible areas, so that Congress and the department then sought to balance this dilution of assistance by a growth point strategy. Thus the next act (1965) required each economic development district, or EDD, to contain at least one urban center of as many as 250,000 people which had "sufficient population, resources, public facilities, industry, and commercial services to ensure that its development [could] become relatively self-sustaining." An injection of new investment into this center would, it was hoped, raise employment and income levels in the surrounding area. In the first three years, sixty-eight EDDs were established (the average population was 181,000) containing about eighty-eight growth centers (with an average population of 38,000).[16] But the diffusion of aid, the lack of direct industrial incentives, and the inability of the federal department to control local planning meant that the "growth point" aim stayed mainly on paper. The program had no real relationship to urban goals.

Simultaneously the policy was broadened further, and state governments entered as direct partners and participants. Political promises to fight rural poverty within the Appalachian hills, which figured in President Kennedy's 1962 election campaign, were followed by congressional creation of the Appalachian Regional Commission in 1965. This commission received substantial funding from Washington, but the thirteen state governors represented on it, along with one presidential appointee, could strongly influence the use of the funds. By working through a small executive committee and employing an able staff, the commission did slightly modify the old public works approach and introduce "human resource development" programs for health, education, and vocational training. Still, the bulk of the funding (about 70 percent) went to highway construction. Overall planning was weakened by interstate bargaining and the region's large amorphous size—it was more than 1,000 miles long and as much as 300 miles wide—which derived from political pressures. Similar pressures caused Congress to provide also for further multistate commissions for economic development, and six such Title V commissions were set up between 1966 and 1972. They were weak copies of the Appalachian concept, with much less money, smaller staffs, and weak overall planning. This provision extended the special aid concept in a diluted form to almost three-quarters of the states in the Union.[17]

Other federal departments, principally Housing and Urban Development (HUD) and to some extent Agriculture, were simultaneously experimenting with special aid programs. HUD administered the 1960s model cities program (see chapter 2), whose coverage was also much widened for political reasons. There was no coordination between the economic development and the urban aid policies. Under congressional acts of 1968 and 1970, HUD was also given responsibility for promoting a very modified version of the European new towns concept. Federal support took the now typical form of mortgage guarantees for land assembly and site preparation by private developers, with supplementary grants for water, sewerage, and open space. In this program, unlike the European, no agencies were established for town building itself, no measures were included for controlling land values, no inducements were available for industry, and no clear links were established with urban growth policies or transportation planning. The 1970 act extended federal support to public agencies, although only two public projects resulted, both developed by a state agency, the New

York State Urban Development Corporation. HUD did not use its own powers to create one or more experimental projects.

HUD had hoped that perhaps ten projects a year would be started, but only fifteen had been funded (partly because of staff shortages in the agency) by 1975, when federal resources became fully occupied with bailing out seven of these projects and refinancing others. By 1978, when the program officially ended, ten projects were still going (two under HUD control), but several were very weak. Financial failures completely killed the program and also bankrupted the New York state agency, and the underlying reasons will be discussed in the last chapter. The program came at an unfortunate time of high inflation and reduced growth rates, when political priorities for central cities were growing. It had a very short trial and could have worked better either earlier or (probably) later in time, as is also suggested by the relative success of a few earlier private new towns such as Columbia (Maryland) and Reston (Virginia), which had no federal support.[18]

Reenter the Central Cities

The third phase of national policies arrived with the growth of unemployment and poverty within old cities. This problem appeared against a background of enormously diffused programs of economic aid. Thus by 1973 more than half the territory of France was an assisted zone, subdivided into three subzones of graded subsidies for industrial relocation and development. By the same year in Britain, three zones of differential assistance (special development areas, development areas, and intermediate areas) covered two-thirds of national territory and 44 percent of population, or more if Northern Ireland is added.[19] In the United States the diffusion of assistance was still greater, albeit on a much smaller scale and without any direct incentives for industrial location. By the late 1970s public expenditure stringency caused these commitments to be scaled down—in Britain, for example, the government in 1979 substantially reduced the areas qualifying for assistance.[20]

How to aid the inner cities? For European countries one obvious question was whether the postwar dispersal policies had been proved mistaken or had become outdated. By 1980 the differences in prosperity and especially in unemployment between the most and the least prosperous regions were again widening; hence this part of the "Barlow policy" might seem as relevant as ever. But still it could be claimed that London and Paris (and a few other cities) had been bled white for the sake of the development areas and, in the British case, for the benefit of a large new town program as well. The new towns were a complicating factor, since they had also enhanced the economic prosperity of some regions (especially those of London and Paris themselves). The issue was whether within a region new towns had been a major cause of inner city problems through their suction of expanding industrial firms and skilled workers. Those who questioned this thesis pointed to the high death rate of firms in inner areas in the 1960s and 1970s and to the fact that new towns absorbed only a small proportion of the people, and a slightly higher one of the firms, who had quit inner areas.

British governments sought to move more resources into the inner cities. The scale of the new town program was reduced in 1978 by lowering their population targets, on the basis that population projections were anyhow falling. The rate support grant to local government was adjusted in favor of big cities. The partnership schemes, described in chapter 2, were not only intended to pinpoint urban spending on the most deprived areas, but were especially concerned with providing financial help for industrial developments and conversions. In France similar policy shifts were occurring.

In the United States there was no planned dispersal policy to reverse, especially given the eclipse of the new communities program. But the enormous volume of unplanned urban sprawl could be attributed partly to the indirect effects of federal policies. The president's national urban policy report for 1978 mentioned four main ways in which these policies bore adversely upon central cities:[21]

1. Lavish Federal financing of the big interstate highway system had facilitated urban dispersal. (Actually the cities had insisted upon participating, and one-third of their traffic movements occurred upon these federal highways, but the central cities seemed to have lost more than they gained from their involvement.)
2. Federal housing mortgages favored suburban residents who were not only wealthier but much better credit risks than inner city residents. Tax concessions on mortgages and low capital gains on land plots had the same effects.
3. Raw land is undervalued for tax purposes, but improvements are overvalued; consequently less incentive exists to invest in inner areas.
4. Federal water and sewerage grants favor sprawl by concentrating on new development and allowing for excess capacity. Central cities have high renewal costs for service infrastructure but receive little more than half as much per head in grants from the Land and Water Conservation Fund.

The urban policies favored by HUD during the 1960s and 1970s sought some modification of the federal inducements which hurt old cities and stimulated urban sprawl. More help for urban public transport aided this goal somewhat, as did the liberalization of mortgages for residents of old and blighted areas, which represented a marked shift of federal policy. There was less success with measures of financial relief. In 1971 a congressional move to offer tax credits to rural industries failed to pass, once the central cities had insisted upon getting the same benefits; suburban interests were strong enough not to be squeezed. The formula for community development block grants was not really favorable to the old central cities, which have dense urban cores.

By 1980 it seemed that urban policies had turned full circle. The certainties of Barlow policies in the postwar European context had weakened, although they left a still powerful legacy of regional aid and development programs. Policies for cities themselves had become confused. Resource priorities had been generally adjusted to funnel rather more financial aid into the inner urban areas, but there was little certainty about the effects or impact of this aid. "Planned dispersal" was under fire, but actual dispersal processes continued and might again accelerate. Broad regional plans lost favor under conditions of retrenchment. Nonetheless, it will be useful next to look at the impact of two such admittedly untypical plans.

London and Paris: The Appeal and Limits of Ambitious Planning

Nowhere has ambitious planning by national governments been carried further than in the capital regions of London and Paris. The two show important differences of history and organization. The London region has a continuous postwar history of evolving plans, but their organizational basis has been flimsy and shifting, whereas regional planning for Paris took off later in the 1960s with a purpose-built organization and a dramatic new plan. The policies are in some respects very different, the British planners favoring far-flung dispersal, which strained the mobility of people and firms, while the French planners favored greater concentration and also aimed to provide the conditions for continuous expansion. Moreover, these are untypical urban regions in both size and political status. But all the same they offer interesting examples of the potential and problems of urban regional planning, as well as crucial tests of the aims of national urban policies.

Abercrombie's *Greater London Plan* appeared in 1944 and complemented the plan also prepared by Abercrombie for the dense urban core then governed by the London County Council. Twenty years later came *The South East Study*, prepared by ministry officials in consultation with local authorities. In 1967 the newly created regional economic planning council presented its *Strategy for the South East*, which led to the tripartite arrangement for regional planning already described. The resulting *Strategic Plan for the South East*, prepared by a joint team led by the ministry's chief planner, came out in 1970, and its first major review appeared in 1976.[22]

These plans took an increasingly broad view of the region to be considered but followed the same guiding concepts. Abercrombie assumed a static total population, following the expert demographic assumptions of that time. Therefore his program represented a once-and-for-all decanting of a surplus population of 1 million and equivalent employment from the congested urban core of London to a ring of new and expanding towns beyond his greenbelt. By the time of the next major plan (1964), demographers were projecting a twenty-year population growth in the region of about 3½ million; but in addition the ministry planners believed that London itself still had the same potential overspill of 1 million people if all prospective households were to be separately housed, if land were to be found for roads, and so forth. The ministry planners might have questioned previous policy, but instead they favored a more extreme solution of developing further and bigger new towns in the outer parts of their planning region, which had been much enlarged to allow for this very conclusion. These seven counter-magnets, located fifty to one hundred miles from London's center, were conceived as large expansions of existing towns which would absorb a big share of regional population growth and would become major ser-vice centers, thereby reducing the dominant pull of the capital, which at that time was especially strong with respect to office employment. Simultaneously the metropolitan greenbelt was to be extended so as to limit further growth within the original new town ring.

The regional planning council believed that the *South East Study* had unrealistically tried to push future growth too far from the capital, and their plan envisaged a series of radial growth corridors running from the outer edge of the greenbelt to the proposed countermagnets, balanced by a radial system of protected green zones. Finally the 1970 regional plan came up with compromise plans for five substantial "growth areas," two of them based upon the original "countermagnets" and three located nearer the capital (but beyond the enlarged greenbelt) along strong lines of radial communications. These five growth areas, while sometimes incorporating new towns, were meant to be looser structures of old and new communities to be planned by the county councils.

These large plans have in fact been implemented to a substantial although diminishing extent by joint action of government and local authorities. The first "Abercrombie" ring of new towns was built by seven new town development corporations (one covering two towns) and by 1980 had absorbed 450,000 people (somewhat beyond the Abercrom-bie target) and was almost completed. It was complemented by a variety of smaller town development schemes, although these were scattered more widely than was originally intended (see chapter 2). The countermagnet concept of the 1964 plan was only partly implemented, but it did lead to one substantial new city (Milton Keynes) and to several more limited developments; in 1980 the government announced that about 330,000 people would eventually move into this outer new town ring, as compared with the 1 million originally projected. Planning for the other substantial and medium-sized growth areas specified in the 1970 plan depends upon the county councils. By 1980 development was proceeding steadily in some of these, but others had been sharply cut back.[23]

An important aim of these projects was to integrate the outward flows of people and jobs, which initially required a speedup of industrial dispersal. London firms were offered industrial sites or advance factories in the new and expanded towns, and the development corporations offered subsidized housing to all workers moving with their firms and also to other persons with suitable skills who were on the waiting lists of the London housing authorities. This policy gave priority to balanced economic development of the new towns rather than to housing those city dwellers in greatest need, although the supply of housing in London gained through the exodus of workers. Subsequently these linkages became weaker, and people and firms moved into the later projects from many places besides London.[24]

Still, the goal of a balanced community was in some respects achieved. The eight original new towns had by the end of 1978 attracted 1,055 industrial occupiers employing 114,000 people, together with more than 500 offices employing perhaps a third as many. In most of these towns there were slightly more local jobs than residents in employment. There was very little commuting to London in comparison with other towns in the metropolitan region, although there were some substantial cross-movements with neighboring and other new towns. There was also less dependence than elsewhere upon one or two large employers. Socioeconomic profiles usually showed some underrepresentation of both the top (managerial and professional) and bottom (unskilled manual worker) classes, especially the latter, a phenomenon due to the preferences of top people for rural retreats and the requirements of incoming firms for skilled labor. The largest imbalance in social structure came from marked age bulges, which resulted from the initial preponderance of young marrieds, although the corporations did later build special housing for elderly relatives.[25]

Constraint policies also had a measure of success. The metropolitan greenbelt was extended to about fifteen miles in depth, and the southeast became blanketed with protected zones—agricultural land of grades 1 and 2, areas of outstanding natural beauty, greenbelts, country parks, National Trust properties, and nature reserves, all together covering about half the land surface. There were many conflicts between conservation and development and between agriculture and recreation, and the conservationists did not always win; but development control was quite strong. The influential and at the time successful minority report of the Roskill Commission by Sir Colin Buchanan argued that these protective measures were so well established and highly valued that the "environmental disaster" of a major airport ought not to be imposed upon any inland site within the southeast.[26]

What have been the general effects of these regional plans upon southeast England?

1. As the research study by Peter Hall and others shows, a principal consequence has been to restrict urban sprawl and protect rural and agricultural areas. A side effect has been to raise land and house prices, although to what extent is unknown.[27]

2. The new towns have been successful in integrating the streams of industrial and population dispersal from the capital, but each new town has been a separate and limited development. Although their sizes have been somewhat enlarged, growth has been pushed elsewhere as each new town approaches completion, and there has been no policy of grouping new towns so as to facilitate continuous development or the creation of strong service centers.

3. There has been substantial decentralization of office employment, produced by the efforts of a government-created advice bureau, by controls on office location in London, and by moves of civil service staff.

4. The countermagnet concept of the 1964 plan has not been realized and seems unlikely to be so (with one possible exception—the new city of Milton Keynes). Basically this result is due to the sharp reduction in expected growth rates, but a contributory factor has been the bias of planning bodies (especially local ones) toward smaller and multiple points of growth.

5. The regional plans have made little positive contribution to the planning of the capital itself. Their function was to absorb the "surplus" growth displaced from London, not to restructure the capital itself, which became a task for the Greater London Council. When growth fell off and the problems of London grew, the role of regional planning inevitably (if perhaps temporarily) withered, but the integration of regional with London planning has been weak except for the acceptance by the regional bodies that more financial aid should be concentrated upon inner areas such as Docklands.[28]

Dramatic changes occurred in the organization and planning of the Paris region during the 1960s. In 1961 a Paris regional authority (now called *la Région d'Ile-de-France*) was created which has comprised since 1968 eight departments (one for the city of Paris, three for the suburbs, four for the outer parts of the region), and which contained initially more than 1,300 communes. This is a natural city region with a 1975 population of nearly 10 million in an area of 4,800 square miles of whom 6.3 million live in the 300 square miles of the central conurbation (Paris and the suburban departments). The region's importance was marked by the appointment of a delegate general as its first regional prefect, by the creation of important technical and research agencies, and by the levying of a special payroll tax to support regional public works. Other regional reforms followed, and Région d'Ile de France now has an indirectly elected council of 164 (50 members of Parliament and 114 local government representatives) and an advisory economic and social council. The regional prefect is in charge of planning and supervises the public institutions for new towns and other regional agencies.[29]

In 1960 the Ministry of Construction prepared a regional plan, which aimed to restrict the growth of employment in Paris through locational controls and decentralization subsidies but rejected new towns or other development projects because of their stimulus to growth. Yet the new delegate general argued strongly that this policy was unrealistic and that Paris ought to be modernized and developed as the premier city of the European Community. As with the *South-East Study* in England, the Paris planners were helped by optimistic growth forecasts which suggested that even if regional development policies were very successful, the Paris region's population would still grow substantially. Because of the expected population and economic growth and changes in tastes, the planners anticipated that by the year 2000 the number of dwellings would double, their total floor space treble, and the surface area they covered quadruple, while there would be equivalent increases in demands for roads, transport, and recreation.

These considerations powerfully influenced the 1965 *Schéma directeur*.[30] This very ambitious plan diagnosed Paris as overcentralized and overcongested. It proposed a number of substantial suburban centers as well as eight new towns on the edge of the capital, each to contain between 0.5 million and 1 million people by the year 2000. Development was to be organized so as to allow for continuous growth around two strong tangential lines of communication extending along the Seine valley to the west and the Marne and Seine valleys to the east. The enormous investment required was not properly costed, although the planners could claim (as in southeast England) that they were only organizing in a farsighted manner investments which would anyhow be required.

The new regional authority moved quickly to implement its plan. A special agency was created for land management and acquisition which by 1977 had placed 133,000 hectares in *zones d'aménagement différé* (ZAD) where land prices are controlled, of which 27,000 hectares had been publicly acquired, half in the new towns. Five new towns were designated which each covered a large area, sometimes as big as the city of Paris, within which were specified major development zones and the sites for large town centers. As in Britain each new town is planned and developed by a corporation appointed by the Minister of Equipment, but the corporation contains local government representatives and works closely with a syndicate of local communes which coordinates services and equalizes local taxes across the new town area.[31]

The budget of the Région d'lle-de-France is larger than all the other French regions combined, partly bcause the region levies both a special payroll tax and the tax on new building. The proceeds are largely devoted to special projects which also utilize national and local finance and are agreed between the three levels of government. The main beneficiary has been transportation, especially the construction of fast new Métro and modernized rail lines connecting the new towns and suburban centers with central Paris. The construction tax has been used to favor suburban centers such as La Défense and new towns as locations for offices, and to favor new towns and (increasingly) inner zones of high unemployment as locations for factories.

Unfortunately, however, the plan's growth assumptions proved seriously mistaken. Whereas the region's population was growing at more than twice the national average in 1954–1962, it fell to just above average in 1968–1975; immigration dried up and natural growth was less than expected. Economic growth was also less, with a still expanding service sector but a slow decline in total industrial jobs. Simultaneously, as with London (though to a smaller extent), decentralization from Paris accelerated, 300,000 people quitting the city itself in 1968–1975, which (as with London) served both to sustain the need for the new towns and to raise questions about their effects on the inner city.

Inevitably development was slower than intended. By 1975 about 150,000 people had moved into the new towns, but their building rates were below half that intended by the plan. Nonetheless the new *Schéma directeur* of 1976 repeated most of the original objectives, albeit with some significant changes in timing and priorities. The new town proposals were pruned from their original great size to projects with intended populations of from 250,000 to 500,000, but the need to concentrate more of the region's housing and limited industrial growth in these towns was strongly affirmed.[32] As with London, a main aim was to prevent urban sprawl, which was in fact more in evidence than the planners liked. The new towns had passed the point of no return, it was claimed, and would soon be strengthened by new educational and medical institutions and the development of strong centers. But simultaneously the claims of the eastern inner zone of the Paris conurbation for more finance and employment were also recognized. The effect of the 1976 plan was to abandon the original stress upon continuous outward growth and to concentrate resources upon existing projects and priority areas and upon the communications which would serve them. Under the impetus of the 1965 plan, Paris took a "leap forward" toward becoming a carefully planned and continuously expanding urban region, but the 1976 plan switched the emphasis toward creating a much enlarged but closely integrated big city.

We now can consider the advantages and limits of urban regional planning on this very broad scale. First, there are many possible gains to be had from strong central government involvement. Boundaries can be more flexible—thus the southeastern planning region of England was enlarged to cover a radius of from forty to more than one hundred miles from London, and the French regional reform was purpose-built for coping with the future growth of Paris. (It was also stronger, more permanent, and more centralized than the flexible London planning system.)

Another advantage is the scope for government initiatives which transcend the political will and financial capacities of local government. The most obvious example is the creation of new towns, which were vital elements in the London and Paris strategies. Among local governments only the London County Council had the administrative and fiscal resources and the political zeal to undertake new town building, and as the Hook case showed, it could not overcome the political opposition to this objective. Then again, central government can use its powers of local plan approval to keep the local authorities in line with the regional plan. But there are, of course, also limits to central government's collective wish to support a plan or to impose its will, a point to which I will return.

Again, strong government involvement carries the hope that regional plans will be coordinated with other national policies such as those for transportation and employment. These hopes have been only partly met. In southeast England, the motorway program has incorporated connections beween the new towns and ports and has given a strong priority to London's outer orbital road, as the regional strategy requires. But airport planning has been much less successful. Although the location of the third London airport is likely to be much the largest factor in urban growth (it is expected to entail £2,000 million in urbanization costs and to influence strongly the location of half a million people), the succession of airport inquiries and regional planning exercises have never been coordinated. Ambitious ideas for a Maplin complex incorporating a vast offshore airport, a new port terminal, and a large urban growth area appealed to the regional economic planning council and to the local authorities but not to the airport planners or the government (which was swayed by considerations of cost). In Paris, de Gaulle airport was better integrated with the regional plan, however.

The socioeconomic as well as environmental impact of a big airport has attracted increasing attention. In Paris the new town of Marne La Vallée was partly designed to house workers at the de Gaulle airport in a noise-free zone, and it was also hoped that the combination of new town and airport would stimulate economic growth in the depressed eastern sector of Paris. Interestingly similar ideas have been advanced about the value of a Maplin airport to the deprived eastern sector of London. The airport (besides having the environmental advantages of an offshore site) would reduce commuting and would provide a strong pole of growth for eastern London, but in 1981 the government was still expressing its long-standing preference for an inland site at Stansted, Essex.[33]

Next, it can be claimed that the policies contained in these plans have some strong advantages, which may only be realized by "positive planning" carried out on a very broad scale. One such is the balancing, integration, and concentration of the processes of urban dispersal. The main instrument here is the new towns, although in the case of Paris the same concept has been fed back into the design of strong suburban centers. The following advantages are often claimed:

1. shortening journeys to work, and facilitating access to new centers or subcenters by public transport
2. protecting the countryside, agriculture, and land reserves by urban compactness and clear boundaries
3. keeping the population and employment flows in balance
4. establishing towns with at any rate greater *potential* for cultural and civic life than exists in diffused suburbs or exurbs.

Earlier new town aims sometimes included an unrealizable goal of a high degree of self-containment. Newer concepts recognize the benefits of mixing substantial local opportunities with access to a major regional center. This aim seems to fit fairly well with information about popular preferences. French and American surveys have shown that many more people would like to move from a big city to a smaller town than vice versa. A French survey found that only 44 percent of the respondents in the Paris conurbation wanted to stay there, and 70 percent thought its growth should be curbed; their strongest objections were to traffic problems, poor public transport, pollution, and noise—a list which makes a case for drastic changes in transportation policy if city life is again to be made acceptable.

A survey for the U.S. Commission on Population Growth and the American Future found that fewer than half the 28 percent living in large urban areas liked that option, whereas life in a small town was much the most popular choice (53 percent of all respondents). A Wisconsin survey pinpointed the issue further by finding that 61 percent preferred small town life, but most of these wanted the town to be within thirty miles of a central city—clear backing for the regional planning principles suggested above. English social surveys have generally showed a high degree of satisfaction among new town residents, whereas many Londoners would like to move out.[34]

Of course, these "preferences" need careful interpretation. The nostalgia of rural emigrants and the nature of retirement goals probably influence the declared preferences of big city dwellers. Significant groups such as young single people have different preferences, and the dissatisfaction of deprived groups in urban ghettoes has deeper causes than regional plans could resolve. Moreover, taken literally the preferences would suggest a degree of antiurbanism which would hardly be satisfied, for example, by the Parisian new towns, although their smaller, more dispersed counterparts in England would score much better. These surveys of opinion also point to the obvious failure of regional plans to treat urban renewal as effectively as they do organized growth or to cope with traffic and transportation in the big cities.

Regional planning of this kind can also be argued to increase economic efficiency. Close physical linkages between firms have become less significant with their increasing size, and in any case journeys must be measured in time as well as distance. It is, for example, often quicker to move thirty miles from a new town to north London than to move ten miles across the capital. Industrial needs for a pool of skilled labor are met to a considerable extent by the development of new towns or groups of related towns. Public expenditure on transportation is relieved by a reduction in the massive daily movement to the central area in favor of smaller movements to substantial subcenters. Working and operating conditions in the new industrial estates bring considerable advantages. The price is the investment in infrastructure required for pushing out the "poles of growth," but the development of medium-sized towns has advantages over further accretions to a big city, especially if the cultural and specialized services of the city are not harmed. Residents in smaller places gain from growth, while big city residents are saved from some of its costs.[35]

There are, however, other respects in which the Paris and London plans can be seriously questioned. These plans would never have gotten off the ground in the 1960s, and certainly not on their actual scale, without demographic and economic forecasts which proved to be wildly wrong. It is curious that the regional planners were able to get away with the argument that these forecasts proved the compatibility of their plans with strong government priorities for other regions. There were strong interdepartmental arguments on the issue in both countries during the 1960s, but the optimistic and politically inspired beliefs in growth were too strong to be shaken. Also, each government accepted the importance of maintaining, and indeed enhancing, the international competitive strength of its capital city. The idea was that the city centers would shed secondary functions to make room for more key functions of international or national importance, but this policy was no help to regional goals if the displaced functions were relocated within the capital regions, as they largely were.

Naturally the plans had to be modified as their assumptions proved seriously false. When it became clear that there was not enough mobile industry to feed the claims of all the growth points in southeast England as well as development areas, some of the former were abandoned. Later the growing inner city problems caused a reduction of the new town programs in both countries. The regional strategies were to some extent saved by another gross error of forecasting, however. While they greatly exaggerated total population growth in both regions, the planners did not anticipate at all the rapid fall in the populations of London and Paris. (The 1 million overspill anticipated in the *South-East Study* was expected only to equal natural increase, leaving London's population static). This spontaneous exodus of population was linked with a sharp fall in household size, and the consequent demand for new dwellings provided a fresh rationale for continuing the development of new towns and growth areas; however, the possible effect of economic recession upon household formation made this rationale in its turn open to question.

From this account, regional planning in London and Paris would appear to have shown a fair degree of continuity and survival value. This is partly because large physical projects have substantial sunken costs—economic, political, and also psychological—so that they are more likely to proceed slowly or be modified than canceled. Then again, a framework of development which has actually won the support or acquiescence of a large number of participants builds up its own momentum and is hard to change. To a point a physical planning strategy can be adapted to slower economic and social change without its basic framework being overthrown; the goals just take longer to realize. This was basically the position taken by the planners both in the first review of the *Strategic Plan for the South East* and in the rewriting of the *Schéma directeur*. Nonetheless the planners were papering over considerable cracks in their edifices. The momentum of regional planning had become much weaker in both cases by 1980.

The London and Paris strategies were significantly different in important respects. The London plans created a wide diffusion of new, relatively small developments, whereas the Paris plans located large new developments very close to the capital; under retrenchment the former approach produced simply weaker growth, and the latter veered toward greater urban concentration and integration. There are historical and cultural explanations for these differences, such as the *urbaniste* traditions of the French and the antiurbanist (or anti–big city) traditions that exist in England as in the United States. There are also empirical reasons, notably the fact that the London region started with a much more developed regional transport system and with more equality in service levels between urban, suburban, and rural areas than the French region had.

The London plans can be criticized for diffusing new growth and the Paris ones for overconcentration. The London new towns are the more definite achievements and seem to accord better with emerging popular preferences in many countries. The countermagnet concept, however, might have been applied with advantage to the economic and cultural development of provincial cities in England as it was in France, even though success in the latter case was limited. In France as in England, however, new growth has in fact increasingly shifted from both Paris and big provincial cities to smaller towns, especially those in the Paris basin. This trend perhaps confirms the assumptions about popular preferences held by English planners.[36]

Finally, there has been a closer relationship between regional planning and the restructuring of the capital itself in the case of Paris. This difference can be ascribed primarily to the urban and cultural factors just noted but also to the fact that the Greater London Council as a big metro authority offers a counterpoise to the influence of regional planning in a way that does not apply to Paris. There the Région d'Ile-de-France acts itself almost as a kind of metro planning agency.

Regional Planning in Federations

The planning of urban regions in federations presents special opportunities and difficulties. The states provide an intermediate layer of government which theoretically should be suitable for this purpose. State governments are usually constitutionally responsible for local government, for direct provision of important services such as highways and health, and for administration of pollution controls and other regulations. Unfortunately, states are often politically reluctant and organizationally ill equipped to perform this role. Sometimes their boundaries are also unsuitable—for example, nine of the thirty largest SMSAs in the United States are multistate. Federal governments have increasingly stepped into this gap, but they lack direct powers, and the problems of coordination arise at both state and federal levels.

In America states are generally reluctant to interfere with the powers or jurisdictions of local governments. Also, the traditional domination of state legislatures by upstate or rural interests (now to some extent rectified) produced unsympathetic state attitudes toward problems of big cities. Recently some states have developed important initiatives in planning, but the main focus of their concern is not urban regions but critical environmental areas such as the California coast, the Florida Keys and Everglades, the Adirondack Mountains (New York), the Rockies (Colorado), the Maine woods, the Delaware coastline, wetlands in many states, and the pleasant countryside of Vermont, threatened by a "second home" boom.

These concerns have led to new powers of state regulation of development, often shared with local governments.[37] For example, Californian coastal protection is overseen by regional commissions, half of whose members are drawn from local government, and development control in Vermont is handled by district environmental commissions of appointed citizens with the possibility of appeal to a state environmental board. Measures have also been passed (for example, the Williamson Act in California) to exclude development value from the tax assessment of agricultural land on condition that no development occurs for a period of years or that a levy is paid when it does so. Hawaii protects agricultural land by a direct zoning law, but generally states pursue environmental (and to a lesser extent agricultural) protection through the medium of general guidelines, not specific plans.

Unfortunately, these state measures often have lopsided effects. They can be used to support the frequently strong opposition of the wealthier local governments to urban growth, although they also, of course, check the tendency of other local governments to put immediate gains before environmental considerations. Frieden describes how selfish suburbanites have coalesced with environmental groups such as the Sierra Club to wall off choice areas of California from development. The rich suburban city of Palo Alto zoned 7,500 acres of rolling foothills (nearly all of its spare land) as open space, even though the city has a surplus of jobs over households and there would seem good reason to encourage more workers to live locally. Marin County, north of San Francisco, refused to expand its water supplies, opposed new highways to give access to its coastal national park, and zoned agricultural land at one house to sixty acres. State planning in California helps such local acts—for example, local tax losses from agricultural protection are compensated by the state, open space protection is subsidized, and the Californian regula- tions with respect to environmental impact statements give strong local groups a powerful instrument for halting any unwanted developments.[38]

In Frieden's view the latent interests of urban dwellers in search of homes have become unfairly outweighed by the overt interests of sub- urbanites and environmental groups. It is clear in any case that the benefits of environmental protection are very unevenly spread and that urban dwellers generally—and poorer ones especially—suffer from the absence of rational plans for urban growth which pay attention to their locational preferences and service requirements. With a few exceptions, such as the Twin Cities metropolitan planning, state planning has not concerned itself greatly with urban regional problems, so that its aims are unbalanced. Metropolitan planning has in consequence hinged upon the financial incentives of the federal government, which have to overcome not only difficulties of local cooperation but the frequently lukewarm or even unhelpful attitudes of state agencies.

On the positive side some states have now made local planning compulsory, and a few have taken steps to review and coordinate local plans. In Oregon since 1973 a commission has reviewed all local plans on the basis of general state guidelines, has fixed broad urban bound- aries and conservation zones, and has been ready to reject a local plan which does not provide for an adequate range and diversity of housing. Other states are beginning to involve themselves in "balanced growth" policies. These accept the case for some curb on growth but seek to distribute volumes and types of development more equitably between localities.

It may be useful to look briefly at the contrasting experience of another federation, Australia.[39] Local government has significantly weaker pow- ers and more dependent status in Australia than in the United States. The big cities are also the state capitals, and each possesses a very high proportion of state population. Nonetheless, as in the United States, state legislatures (especially the upper house) have accorded disproportionate weight to rural interests. This fact, and the strong opposition to planning by property interests in the central cities, discour- aged state governments from developing planning frameworks until 1945 and sometimes later. At first, planning was done on a limited scale by generally small urban governments under the supervision of a state department.

The planning frameworks devised by states represent differing concepts of "partnership" between state and local government and of coordination among the state agencies themselves. The most localized framework comprised the Cumberland County Council (1945), covering 1,750 square miles and comprising ten members elected by the thirty-nine local governments in Greater Sydney, which was specifically set up to prepare and oversee a regional planning scheme. Metropolitan planning was here given local roots at the insistence of the local governments, but the council was abolished in 1963. Melbourne is the scene of a curious compromise whereby the Melbourne and Metropolitan Board of Works, a water and sewerage authority indirectly elected by local governments but with a state-appointed chairman, was handed the task of metropolitan planning by the Victorian state government in 1949 and had its planning area trebled in 1968. Still, the more usual arrangement has been the creation of a state planning authority comprising officials from key state departments and agencies, representatives of local government, and sometimes also representatives of professional and business interests. Such bodies were established in Western Australia (1959), New South Wales (1963), and South Australia (1967) in order in particular to deal with the planning of Perth, Sydney, and Adelaide, respectively.

These state planning authorities have varying powers to prepare a metropolitan plan, to control local planning by regulations, to override local decisions on key matters, and sometimes also to control land subdivision, protect scenic areas, and exercise other direct powers. Local government tends to be much the junior partner in these arrangements. Another purpose of the arrangement is to coordinate the many state departments or "independent" agencies concerned with roads, public transport, housing, industrial development, water, sewerage, and other utilities. Problems of coordination were one main reason for the eclipse of the locally controlled Cumberland County Council, but state planning agencies still face formidable obstacles to an effective integration of urban development policies. One reason is the long-standing compartmentalism and independence of the various state bureaucracies, a phenomenon which is equally marked in the United States. Another reason is the intrinsic difficulties of achieving integration through the instrumentality of a statutory land use plan.[40]

Metropolitan planning for Sydney and Melbourne has not much affected the intensification of development and employment in their city centers, combined with low-density sprawl at their peripheries. The Cumberland County Council produced the boldest plan for Sydney (1951), but its Abercrombie-like proposals for a greenbelt and the decentralization of employment were not realized. Later plans accepted the desirability of urban growth and concentrated upon controlling its directions, but at a price of offering a "punters' guide" for land specula-tors and of probably widening locational inequalities. In these two cities, however, and still more in Adelaide, proposals for urban freeways were quashed or much modified through environmental opposition, and transportation planning at state and city level has become better coor-dinated. Crude policies for intensive urban redevelopment have also been quashed, and in Adelaide the South Australian Housing Trust planned and developed a satellite town and is doing the same for a big new regional center.[41] The experience of state metropolitan planning in Australia is not wholly negative, and an institutional framework for its development exists which could be improved. On the other hand, efforts to strengthen local government, such as the Cumberland County Coun-cil and the various proposals for a metro government in Melbourne, have been thrust aside.

At the federal level the Whitlam Labour government (1972–1975) followed the Kennedy-Johnson example of coming to the rescue of the cities. Special aid was funneled to disadvantaged areas, which in the Australian context meant poorly serviced suburbs in the west of Sydney and Melbourne. Regional organizations of local governments were formed to coordinate aid, but their powers and potential ability for planning were slight. The larger Labour initiatives included financial inducements to the states to establish new growth centers, and to set up state land commissions with powers to buy, service, and sell or lease land. A new Department of Urban and Regional Development (DURD) was created with a very broad remit. Progress with these radical initia-tives was patchy because of the need for cooperation from the states and also because of conflicts between DURD and Treasury. These pro-grams have been gradually run down by the subsequent Fraser govern-ment, although one major growth center (Albury-Wodonga) and some land commissions have survived in a rather truncated form.[42] This ex-perience seems to confirm that in Australia federal action has to pro-ceed through inducements to the states to undertake more effective metropolitan planning.

In Germany the "fiscal federalism" of the United States and Australia is less marked, and the constitution distributes legal competence be-tween governmental levels according to its degree of generality. The federal government can therefore establish a broad legal framework for urban planning, although the main responsibility rests with the *Länder*. Hamburg and Bremen are effectively city states, and Hamburg has adopted a comprehensive system of land use, transportation, and in-frastructure planning, although it is losing population to surrounding

Länder because of narrow boundaries. Hamburg has also used its higher status to help other German cities cope with central and state controls over their plans.[43]

The Evaluation of Regional Planning Systems

Regional planning frameworks have emerged through a convergence of issues that have been remitted to this level from below and above. Local governments have needed to cooperate in order to cope with the facts of urban growth and change. They have often been reluctant to do so, and central governments have intervened to foster local government cooperation or reorganization. Simultaneously, national economic and urban policies have required central governments to strengthen their regional machinery for interdepartmental coordination and planning.

The consequences have been a luxuriant growth of regional planning frameworks. Sometimes these frameworks have been ad hoc, the aim being primarily the preparation of a regional plan; more often they are permanent or have a degree of flexible continuity. There are also frameworks for different purposes which may be coordinated weakly or not at all. In the United States separate regional frameworks have been established for transportation, water resources, air pollution control, health, multicounty and multistate economic development, and metropolitan planning. By contrast, in many unitary states multipurpose systems of coordination have been established which try to integrate the activities of central departments and local authorities and sometimes (though usually more weakly) public corporations and special agencies as well.

It will be convenient first to consider the strengths and weaknesses of these "partnership" systems of multiorganizational cooperation while recognizing that their details vary substantially.

1. These frameworks, as noted in the last section, bring together a large number of organizational actors, a feature which in principle should produce a comprehensive degree of cooperation. Still, this advantage is offset by a low degree of organizational commitment to the regional planning body. The regional civil servants are primarily responsible to their central departments, and local government representatives and officials answer to their local constituencies.
2. Political legitimacy and visibility of the regional organizations is weak. The appointment of an advisory body introduces a representative, or "lay," element which strengthens the regional machinery and stiffens the willingness of departmental or local government officials to act cooperatively. All the same, without a clear electoral base and constituency, political legitimacy is likely to be low, and the workings of the

regional machinery are terra incognita to most citizens and a source of suspicion to many elected representatives.

3. Regional systems have no or few resources directly under their control. Resource allocation is determined by the central machinery of government and by the priorities of individual departments and local authorities. The weakness of its political legitimacy and organizational autonomy largely disqualifies a regional body from raising or spending money.

4. Paradoxically these very political and organizational limitations can actually strengthen the capacity of a regional body to make imaginative plans. The very variety of organizational interests involved reduces the pull of any one interest. The absence of any controlling elected body removes an impediment to joint planning between different levels of government. (This fact explains the frequent preference of administrative reformers for *advisory* regional councils; these confer legitimacy and can offer useful advice but do not wield power). In these circumstances the planning staff may be able to take a more detached and objective view of regional issues than would otherwise be possible. This gain is a contingent one—it will only occur if there is sufficient consensus among participants over the need for such planning. Political and organizational rivalries do not disappear at the regional level—they are only more muted or latent, making independent initiatives more practicable. The professional planners themselves can contribute imaginative ideas only if there is some consensus among the participants and/or strong support from a higher authority.

Regional machinery in Britain and France has been described in this chapter. The description above applies much more obviously in the former than the latter case. It may indeed be objected that in France the regional institutions have acquired both political importance and organizational effectiveness. Regional reform was a major although unachieved goal of President de Gaulle, and a modified reform was subsequenty introduced in 1972. Yet, the French regional system still displays in considerable degree the kinds of weakness listed above. The regional council is only indirectly elected, and its taxing and spending powers are extremely small. In the metaphysic of the French state, the region is not even a "territorial organization" (a term reserved for the traditional *départements* and communes) but only another public institution. This terminology indicates the limited political legitimacy, and rather low political visibility, of the French regions.

Certainly the new French regional machinery reflects the highly integrated character of French government administration. The département prefect was always a key coordinator of both government departments and local governments, although his actual capacities in this respect have always (and indeed increasingly) been a good deal less than his formal powers. The introduction of the regional prefect and linked regional institutions (the elected council, the advisory council, and the interdepartmental conference) carries this concept of integrated administration to a higher regional level. The region is a center of decision making in the sense that primarily because of the role of its prefect, a variety of pressures from above and below (both political and administrative in character) can be absorbed and to some extent resolved at that particular level. This gives the regional institutions some leverage for regional planning, but leverage that hinges primarily upon a crossroads position within a multitiered framework of collective decision making, not upon an independent political and resource base.

Lacking any equivalent to the prefect, the English regional machinery was dependent upon the sponsorship of one Whitehall department whose primacy in regional affairs was far from unquestioned. Once the Department of Economic Affairs had failed as an overall coordinator, its successor, the Department of the Environment, had limited capacity to integrate at the regional level such strong rival interests and priorities as those of the Department of Industry. Hence the English regional machinery became far more a vehicle for guiding the plans of local governments than was the case in France, and for this reason (and because of facts of regional geography) its influence bore more directly upon the planning of urban regions. There were proposals for moving also toward a French system of indirectly elected councils, although in the English context such bodies would have had a much more distant relationship with the government departments than the regional advisory councils enjoyed. The English dilemma was that these councils had influence only to the extent that ministers were actively keen on regional planning, and that their educational role vis-à-vis local government could not last indefinitely. Their existence seemed to lead nowhere—hence they could easily be axed in an economy drive—although in fact they were important for the degree of regional integration which was achieved.

The regional plans for London and Paris form exceptions to the general weakness of regional machinery, primarily because of the special interest of the central governments in the fortunes of their capital cities. Government departments concerned with urban and physical planning usually give a disproportionate amount of their time to the capital city. Even when policies for containing the growth of European capitals were fully dominant, it was still regarded as essential to resolve the problems of London or Paris if other regions were to be helped. Moreover, these problems were much more palpable and important at a national political level than were those of other big cities.

For London there is a long history of ministerial efforts to get cooperation among the local planning authorities, which led finally to the formation of the Standing Conference on South-East Regional Planning. The responsible government department (now the Department of the Environment) played a critical part in both the making and the implementation of regional plans. The Abercrombie plan went through the hurdles of revision by both a joint local government and an interdepartmental committee, and the resulting document was issued as official policy. On this occasion as subsequently, for example, in the case of the *South-East Study,* the issues were regarded as too important to be stalled by subsequent foot-dragging from other departments, although this activity did of course occur. The new towns legislation and the legislation for development control in rural areas passed and were implemented with the problems of London primarily in view. The local authorities were kept in line to a considerable if never complete extent by ministerial review of their development plans. This monitoring was helped at a later stage by advice on local plans from the regional council. Nonetheless, the system did gradually run down, partly because the central department became less prepared to override the local councils or to use its own strategic powers such as new town designations and partly because regional problems acquired lower salience as those of London grew. Nonetheless, the long tradition of regional planning and local government cooperation which has grown up in the London and southeast region remains a strong asset not yet to be found elsewhere.

The Paris experiment differed in that it came much later and rested more strongly upon specific regional institutions. This institutional base and the absence of any countervailing metro authority like the GLC has helped regional planning. Nonetheless, the continuous support of central agencies was as important as in London; for example, DATAR had to be brought to accept the importance of restructuring Paris for the sake of its international role. Also, the number of local communes makes their coordination more difficult and increases the likelihood of significant deviations from regional aims at the local level. The London and Paris plans are of general interest primarily as they tell us about the possible aims and scope of regional planning, but as examples of coordinative machinery they are doubtful guides to what may be practicable elsewhere because of their special importance and great size.

In federations two constitutionally independent levels of government are concerned with urban regions. The system works well only where a state government, for reasons of geography and politics, is prepared to operate itself or to initiate effective planning for the urban region. So far there are few examples in the United States of successful state initiatives of this kind, although the situation may well change. In Australia the states have necessarily accepted much more responsibility for metropolitan planning, although as yet with very limited and variable effectiveness. While federal governments have for political reasons become increasingly involved with the cities' problems, they have in fact a very weak legal capacity for improving metropolitan planning. Their only tool is money—the uses of "fiscal Federalism."

In the United States federal money for research and planning has been plentiful. It has been funneled through multiple regional frameworks—the Appalachian and multistate planning commissions, the commissions for river basin planning, the metropolitan planning agencies, the regional transportation bodies, and others. The impact of all this planning activity has actually been rather slight. The basic reason is that the states and local governments participate in planning primarily to obtain the federal money rather than because they want to use the plans. Thus although many interesting studies have been done (as well as many that are very flimsy and hasty), planning is a somewhat ritualistic exercise. When the money has been received, it is time to turn to the next exercise.

A great weakness of the United States regional frameworks is the difficulty of coordinating the federal agencies themselves. Thus the Appalachian and Title V commissions spend their resources mainly upon "topping up" specific federal grants that are already available, an activity which has little effect upon the priorities and policies of the grant-giving agencies themselves. The federal Office of Management and Budget (OMB) is suspicious of any joint federal-state agency which is liable to function mainly as a device for prising open the federal pursestrings. Still, OMB has been supportive of specific planning frameworks, for example, those concerned with water resources, where a federal agency takes the lead. Despite OMB's backing, the main instrument for achieving general coordination among federal agencies themselves—the federal regional councils comprising regional directors of major departments—has been quite ineffective. The fragmented character of federal administration makes it hard to secure cooperation between the bureaus in one department, let alone between departments. Regional councils are devices for making minor adjustments to decisions, not planning bodies.[44]

On the other hand, if states and local governments were to work out satisfactory frameworks for metropolitan planning, federal financial aid could have an enormous influence upon the kind of planning undertaken. HUD's experiments in trying to combat urban poverty through closely monitored categorical grants are largely ended, but in any case the sums involved were rather insignificant compared with the total impact of federal tax and expenditure policies upon cities. A federal urban strategy could by stages influence the pattern of this expenditure and could thereby influence state policies toward the cities.

This possible phase of federal policy was in fact approached in Australia during the Whitlam era, although the experiment was short-lived and truncated. It can only take deeper roots, as the Australian experience showed, if a greater degree of coordination among federal agencies can be achieved and if the objectives of such a policy can achieve at least some sustained political support—admittedly most difficult conditions.

This section has concentrated upon the organizational and political weakness of regional planning frameworks. This weakness can be traced to the problems of coordinating government departments on the one hand and of building partnerships between central and local government on the other. The problems differ according to the strength of different governmental levels and to the extent of pluralism or integration within the governmental system.

The fact that coordination of a large number of agencies is intrinsically difficult presents performance in a different light. For example, the degree of cooperation actually realized in France would seem utopian by American standards. The criteria of success may need to be modest inasmuch as the prizes of successful regional planning are potentially much greater than those within the more limited grasps of cities and metros. But this discussion of regional planning frameworks bring us back full circle to the question of what planning can hope realistically to accomplish—to which the last chapter turns.

5: The Planning of Urban Regions

Planning Aims and Horizons

It has to be recognized that the actual form of organization—whether city, metro, or regional body—makes only a limited difference to planning policies. Differences in national systems of public powers and policies are likely to be more significant, but again, those national differences need to be related to political and economic changes, and to shifts in beliefs and ideas, which affect all Western societies. I have given many examples of policy changes—for example, in housing and transportation policies—which have occurred at much the same time in many different societies. A full examination of the causes of public policy change lies beyond the scope of this book, but in this section it will be useful to stand back from the organizational framework of the last three chapters and consider more broadly what sort of support for public planning might be available in the future.

Let us consider first the social and political changes in Western European countries in the light of theories discussed in chapter 1. After World War II there was a heavy dependence upon collective consumption. A large majority depended upon public transport, and a majority of those demanding new housing expected government to provide it. Large numbers of industrial workers looked to governments to improve their environmental conditions and to distribute fairly the jobs which, it was expected, would be assured by Keynesian full employment policies. Urban planning could to some extent ride the tide of these welfare goals. If it could help to deliver these goods while improving the quality of life in towns and cities, it could expect at least a passive majority support.

Today in these countries a majority of families own cars and a large, increasing proportion (sometimes, as in England, a majority) own their own dwellings. There is increased privatization of consumption and less effective demand for or pride in civic and communal facilities except of a prestigious or tourist-attracting nature. The concentrations of industrial populations in old urban areas have been significantly dispersed and partly replaced by immigrants with different needs and less articulate political demands. Suburbanization and technological change have weakened the homogeneity of the "working class" and have produced increasing social and occupational differentiation. Planning has lost its association with mass demands for collective consumption and urban betterment or with the interests of an underprivileged majority. Today's deprived groups consist of minorities making uncoordinated demands, and the dominant majority (insofar as one can be discerned) is tilted upward in the income scale.

Admittedly this description is an oversimplification. It would be false history to suggest that urban planning as such was ever a mass cause, being too esoteric for this purpose. It always derived much of its support from suburban and rural groups concerned with their amenities and from individual enthusiasts, philanthropists, and pioneers. Nonetheless, the interests of a latent majority in environmental betterment, economic redistribution, and collective consumption provided essential support and a powerful impetus to postwar planning which has gradually been dissipated.

Next we should consider the relations between the economic system and planning policies. Galbraith and other writers have pointed to the role of governmental planning in ensuring adequate and profitable markets for private business. Neo-Marxist theorists explain the function of planning to be that of "bailing out" a monopoly capitalist system with decreasing scope for profitable markets, through the provision of infrastructure, public contracts, collective consumption for workers, and other financially unprofitable activities. The growth of these state functions is alleged to produce a fiscal crisis which cannot be solved as long as the profitable sector of the economy must be left to the diminishing capacities of private capital.[1] It is a common feature of these theories that government planning encounters a tripwire of the requirements of capitalism which cannot be breached without bringing down the whole system. This constraint applies as much at the local as at the national level, so that local government will be obliged to respond to the demands of private business or developers. The less the scope for profitable activities, the stronger will be this latent compulsion. The effect of this structural constraint is to increase urban inequalities through the priority given to business and financial interests.

These structural theories offer alternatives to the explanations for the causes of urban inequality that are provided (or might be deduced) from theories of elitism or pluralism. It would seem, in fact, that the latter theories are quite capable of explaining the frequent influence of business interests in terms of their capacity for political leverage and the need for their financial contributions. Conversely, structural theories are not good at explaining the cases where, in some cities at least, local planning seems to have been indifferent to business interests and much more concerned with environmental goals expressed in population, housing, and other targets. Structural theories deny or minimize the variable impacts of local politics and the ideas of planners themselves.

Still, we need not swallow these theories wholesale to accept the notion that planning is strongly and increasingly circumscribed by the functioning of the economic system. The international mobility of capital attenuates the practicality of controls over the location of new industries. Competition grows for mobile sources of investment and employment. The concentration of enterprises and the specialization of production make urban areas more economically dependent upon a few large sources of employment and upon branch firms whose headquarters are located elsewhere. Fiscal needs make cities less able and willing to relate the demands of private firms and developers to wider social goals and leave them with fewer resources to pursue those goals. These trends reduce the capacity of planning authorities to exercise influence over economic developments and make them more vulnerable to the consequences of economic contraction.[2] Some of both the successes and failures of postwar urban planning in Europe were linked to political and economic conditions which no longer apply. One example is the close link between planning and housing policies discussed in chapter 2.

The public housing sector, like the home ownership sector, has expanded rapidly in many countries, in both cases at the expense of private renting. But the economic advantages of home ownership have grown faster because of inflation and tax concessions on mortgages, while the quality and social status of public housing has fallen. Public programs have been curtailed everywhere and houses sometimes sold off to tenants. Local governments have less ability to control the provision and location of private housing. Projects like new towns have lost much of their original rationale as contributions to the public housing problems of cities. The high proportions of public housing in both the English and French new towns is not essential, and they could be built mainly on the basis of home ownership. But their historical development does affect their political identification. Public planning has to be made acceptable to the dominant interests of homeowners.

A second example is employment policies. Initially it was possible through incentives and controls to steer mobile industries and offices to both vulnerable regions and new towns. There were always limits to these policies, however, and in a period of recession the shortage of mobile enterprise frustrates the aims of planning. Priorities become confused through the increase of regional and local competition for industries and financial aid. These competitive pressures are funneled through an increasingly elaborate planning process in European countries, whereas in the United States there is more overt competition between localities. But if government resources become scarce, priorities have to be more carefully selected and new methods have to be found for promoting employment.

It can be hypothesized that European countries have now moved into the conditions of political pluralism and of a dominant majority drawn from the more affluent and mobile groups, which had developed thirty years sooner in the United States. But the comparison could be misleading because of the decline or disappearance of economic growth and a general shift in social values and beliefs. In the 1950s and 1960s Americans trusted in economic and technological development to produce social progress and harmony and saw little need for public planning. Planners themselves subscribed indiscriminately to the values of increased individual mobility and opportunities without worrying about the limits to this aim or its likely effect upon community life. Some writers seemed to be so mesmerized by these prospects, that they viewed planning as simply a forecasting and monitoring device for the provision of more and more physical facilities. This rather mindless trend in planning was followed by the counter-attack of Marxist writers who could point to facts of social conflicts and inequalities.

Today these beliefs in the beneficence of technology and in the value of an indefinite extension of personal mobility are taking some sharp knocks. A book such as Peter Hall's *Great Planning Disasters* illustrates the gross errors which these assumptions bring about. The case studies of the third London airport and the London urban motorways reveal the folly of transportation plans based upon forecasts of excessive demand which paid too little attention to social and environmental effects—and which, once passions were aroused, were canceled or indefinitely postponed. The cases of the Anglo-French supersonic Concorde and BART in the San Francisco bay area show, although in different ways, the folly and expense of relying upon advanced technology to solve complex problems. The folly of the Concorde was unrelieved—it was an absurd way of combating Britain's problems of economic and political decline, which could be its only basic justification. The folly of San Francisco's transit system was qualified, because the basic goal of improving public transport was socially and economically justifiable, and the mistake lay in reliance upon an unproven and expensive technology of the wrong kind. (More conventional public transport and traffic restraint were probably the only realistic means to achieve the system's goals).[3]

If there is to be any positive planning in the future, then it will have to satisfy the conditions sketched in chapter 1. Organizational issues aside, there has to be an adequate political base, and issues have to be identified, perceived, and analyzed in ways which require new and more comprehensive policy solutions. We can at least note some changes in issue perception which might facilitate these developments.

First, there are the pressures of the environmental movement. The support of the more affluent and mobile groups continues to be available for planning measures concerned with the conservation of wild, attractive, or vulnerable rural areas, the protection of historic houses and nature reserves, the development of recreational resources, and the control of urban and industrial development. These measures are often negative—they seek to ward off or divert growth. Purely negative environmental measures are unlikely to succeed in the long run, because they have no answer to the pressures of population growth, smaller household sizes, and the demands of many urban dwellers for better housing and a better living environment. The answer sometimes given by environmentalists, that cities should be redeveloped more intensively in order to absorb these pressures, is quite unrealistic, and grossly unfair in terms of the distribution of living space.

Yet environmental and urban interests could come to a reasonably satisfactory mutual accommodation. They could both benefit from plans which provide an adequate volume and range of housing opportunities while protecting sensitive environmental areas, seek a reasonably economical use of energy and land, and concentrate facilities and simplify access patterns. There are very general prescriptions, no doubt, but a piecemeal process of urban growth produced by a mixture of market forces and very localized political pressures seems likely to be less efficient and equitable than a balanced plan for urban growth. In any event it seems impossible to pursue environmental planning effectively or fairly without marrying it to comprehensive urban planning. It might therefore be possible to reestablish or to initiate the kind of tacit coalition between urban and rural interests which underpinned planning legislation in postwar Britain.

Second, there is growing awareness of the need to balance and integrate the opportunities available to different social groups. The concept of "maximizing individual opportunity" cannot be removed from its social context because more opportunity for some means less for others, and generally it is the weaker groups who suffer. For example, urban growth patterns which suit affluent and mobile male heads of households are often much less satisfactory for working wives or old people. The opportunity to drive a car without restriction in cities is in conflict with the opportunities available to those who need or wish to utilize public transport. Or, to take another example, the opportunity to practice small-scale or part-time farming or horticulture—an opportunity which has much to commend it under conditions of shorter working hours and more unemployment—is in conflict, at least in European countries, with the interest of agribusiness in maximizing food production. Thus if planning stands—as it often claims to do—for "maximizing individual opportunities," it must increasingly work to reconcile these requirements.

Third, there is the relationship between individual and communal values. Very often there need be no conflict. For example, an individual's wish for self-expression through the development of his house and garden seems to be perfectly congruent with active participation in community life—in fact, Stretton contends that the two activities are mutually supportive.[4] On the other hand the search for what Fred Hirsch calls "positional goods" such as second homes, second (or third) cars, and higher occupational or educational status is to some extent self-defeating, because the rewards of a higher status cannot be diffused (people have to move upward to occupy the same relative position) and because of physical congestion which can only be remedied at high cost.[5] At the same time the privatization of consumption can be carried to a point where it may have an adverse effect upon community life.

An important aspect of community life is the state of the public domain. The public domain comprises the streets, subways, parks, public buildings, and other facilities which belong in principle to all citizens. This domain may be well or badly designed or maintained, and it may be cherished or neglected by citizens. Today the public domain is deteriorating not simply, or even primarily, because of stringency in public expenditure (Galbraith's "private affluence and public squalor") but because privatization of consumption and divergence of individual lifestyles causes neglect or dislike and fear of communal activities and meeting grounds. Yet it is in everyone's interest, including that of the most successful, to have a safe and attractive public environment.

Indeed, the concept of the public domain may need to be greatly extended so as to comprehend a basic public responsibility for the satisfactory maintenance of common resources of air, water, land, and energy. Such an extension of responsibilities cannot rest simply upon piecemeal regulations but needs some view or vision of the purposes of public planning and of the resources (political and economic) necessary to sustain it. Even if the views of "ecodoomsters" are much exaggerated, the potential exhaustion of many natural resources, and the political dangers of excessive reliance upon overseas sources of supply, strengthen the case for balanced measures of conservation within urban regions.

Some of these points can be illustrated from David Popenoe's comparison of the opinions of their inhabitants (twenty years later) about two developments built in the 1960s—Vallingby, one of Stockholm's planned satellites, and Levittown, in Bucks County, Pennsylvania. The comparison is the more interesting because both developments occurred in rich, capitalist countries and were of similar size, yet one was comprehensively planned and largely built by the city itself, while the other was the product of a successful mass housing entrepreneur.[6]

Levittown is home-centered and its residents are generally well satisfied with their homes and gardens, but it is basically a large housing estate. Workplaces and shopping are scattered, social facilities are inadequate, and movement depends wholly on the car. Vallingby is less home-centered; its garden apartments (the most usual housing type) are pleasant and acceptable but less used or valued than the Levittown houses. Access to shops and workplaces is safe and convenient, local social facilities are excellent, and the public domain (unlike Levittown's) is safe, attractive, and extensively used for cycling, walking, and other pursuits. Levels of satisfaction seemed to be very high in Vallingby, but less so in Levittown, where there were complaints from working wives and teenagers about problems of access and lack of anywhere to go and where some families felt economic pressure to maintain their homes and cars.

Too much cannot be made of one case study, and perhaps Swedes are less critical or less ambitious than Americans. Also, Vallingby is a good example of a "planned development," and it is particularly well suited to small households (larger families have tended to move out). One case does not prove the superiority of planning over market enterprise, but it does support the value of making balanced provision for the needs of different social groups. It also shows the value of a safe and attractive "public domain" (including good public transport) for sustaining a satisfactory community life. Both goals require planning.

Clearly it is not easy to make the maintenance of community structure and diversity a goal of planning, nor could such a goal be pursued in defiance of individual tastes. Yet it seems reasonable for planning to try to preserve or create a wider range of choice (in terms of housing, jobs, and environmental conditions) than would exist under conditions of increasing market specialization and to seek to maintain or introduce those communal facilities which improve community life and social integration. Thus the case for planning will rest in part upon increased awareness of the dangers of social disintegration and divisiveness. It may be that another "tragedy of the commons" is taking place—an erosion of communal resources which matches that of natural resources. If so, measures which can help to avert this tragedy are even more important in the social than the environmental field.

Of the values discussed in chapter 1, that of "community control" is well entrenched in the practice of planning, especially, but not only, in the United States. The value of local autonomy has genuine and considerable appeal in an era of big government and bureaucracies. Still, it can be and frequently is used for narrowly self-regarding purposes at the expense of broader considerations of efficiency, equity, and environmental planning as well. The slogan "no room in the lifeboat," displayed tacitly or overtly by rich communities and their allies, is not an appealing one. Local management of public services and some local discretion over the use of resources are desirable principles, but local policymaking on issues featuring a high degree of mutual interdependence seems less defensible. Institutional reform, further discussed in subsequent sections, does represent one important instrument for strengthening the political base of planning.

Yet an appeal to broader constituencies is by no means a sufficient solvent for providing that base. The latent interests of larger majorities which can thereby be invoked may not necessarily prevail over narrower but more overt and well-organized interests. Relatively enlightened policies can still be applied in ways which spread their costs and benefits very unequally. Thus the problem still remains of winning majority support for a program which tackles the now deep sources of urban inequalities.

If the structural theories of capitalist domination are correct, no answer can be offered to this problem. It may be, however, that they are sufficiently wrong for some answer to be found in terms of the enlightened self-interest of the majority. It would be necessary to convince this majority that a more positive exercise of state planning could simultaneously achieve substantive and redistributive aims which taken together would be beneficial. A measure of redistribution would be paid for, so to speak, by greater overall satisfactions as well as through the reduction of social tensions. This proposition, like all of this section, is necessarily speculative, but in this short space the aim has been no higher than to suggest that the case for some comprehensive degree of urban planning, discussed in chapter 1, is still alive, despite changed political and economic conditions.

The Working of Planning Systems

There are a bewildering variety of planning systems, but for our purposes three general forms need to be analyzed—those of framework planning, corporate planning, and (potentially at least) the concept of strategic planning.

Framework planning is concerned with trying to guide, influence, and coordinate the decisions made by a variety of actors both public and private. It occurs variously at national, regional, and local levels. It is in principle comprehensive, although its effective range may be limited. Economic and environmental plans of a broad-based character are the most familiar types of framework planning.

In many European countries there are now elaborate frameworks for physical or environmental planning. At the national level general guidelines are laid down which amount in one or two cases (for example, that of the Netherlands) to an outline physical plan; at the regional or provincial level, general strategies or outline plans are prepared; at the next level of large local governments, general structure plans are prepared; while at the most local level come the specific plans regulating land use in detail or providing the legal basis for large public projects. Thus in many countries one can distinguish four levels of such planning: besides the national level (a common factor) there are in England the regional strategies, the county structure plans, and the local plans or action plans for public projects prepared usually by district councils although sometimes by counties; for the Netherlands there are the provincial plans, the plans for big cities or subregions, and the plans for local regulation and action prepared by municipalities; for Germany there is planning by the states (Länder), by districts which comprise a group of local authorities coordinated by the Land, and by the municipalities; for France there are the regional plans, urban master plans for conurbations and cities, and detailed plans for the regulation of land uses. The actual situation can be even more complicated, as there may be other levels of planning in addition to those described.

Within the United States there is a still richer luxuriance of planning activities, but there is no hierarchy of general framework plans such as occurs in European countries. There are the multistate economic planning commissions, but their scope is more limited than their title. Physical planning is done by individual local governments usually without the guidance of general framework plans laid down by higher levels of government except for the shadowy influence of jointly produced metropolitan plans. Planning in the United States has a strong organizational basis in the specific aims of government departments or other public bodies, and while many interorganizational frameworks for planning exist, these are nearly always weak, partial, and unrelated to each other.

The advantages of these complex planning frameworks are familiar. They enable planning to relate (in theory at least) to organizational cooperation at multiple levels. They place detailed local plans within broader subregional, regional, and national contexts, thus at least facilitating more consistent and coherent planning policies. They help to avoid the narrow localism or parochialism which governs land use planning in the United States. The introduction of a regional dimension has been of value for its perspective upon urbanization and the emergence of city regions. Yet the elaboration of planning systems also brings new problems and confirms (or disguises) some old ones.

First, the planning cycle is long and slow, yet it is still not definitive. The plans often do not appear in logical sequence, and the status of the various plans or the significance of national guidelines is often not clear. Even the statutory local plan is less than binding, since its application often permits considerable administrative discretion and it is possible for developers to appeal against its provisions to a review board or higher authority. Public as well as private developers (especially big ones), not infrequently manage to make a hole in the elaborately constructed planning process.

Second, physical planning tends in practice to be somewhat passive, narrow, and legalistic. Private developers will only do what the plan seeks to achieve if more positive inducements and instruments of management are available than a regulatory document. Public developers are guided largely by quasicommercial criteria and often operate on a large scale through national or regional public corporations.

Third, the planning process is (naturally enough) infused with politicial and organizational bargaining. As chapter 1 indicated, the inputs into policymaking are subtly shifted through the introduction of more comprehensive kinds of planning. Framework planning introduces broader constituencies (political and organizational) to correct the narrow political base of purely local planning. It also serves to articulate different interests at each level—for example, those of districts and counties in English local government. In theory a disaggregation of national policy goals would occur as planning moves downward and an aggregation of interests take place as the process moves upward. In practice the system is too weak and incoherent for such a logical result, but the planning process can be strongly permeated by pluralist bargaining between major interests. Each type or level of plan becomes, then, a position statement on behalf of some interest, as Castells suggests in his analysis of local and regional planning in northeast France.[7]

The political element in the planning process is of course no intrinsic defect of the system. But it is a problem that planning occurs weakly at multiple levels, because this reduces the scope for establishing a coherent policy at any level. Equally weakened is the scope for public participation by any groups of citizens who lack a material interest in the outcome. The importance of physical planning to owners of property is a major reason for the elaboration of statutory procedures of participation exercises, public inquiries, reviews of plans, and rights of appeal. Yet these procedures have become so complex that they confer a major advantage upon those interests which can profit from a long and costly process of review and arbitration. It is true that the planning process has also had increasing inputs from voluntary bodies and citizens' groups, but this is mainly a witness to the increasing hostility which development proposals arouse. The planning process as now designed does not produce much of that positive participation by citizens over planning the future of their community which it is supposed to bring forth.[8]

We must next consider the relevance of *corporate planning*. This concept is rooted in the goals of an organization, and particularly in its efficient use of available resources. Its basis therefore seems more realistic than that of framework plans which hinge upon a considerable degree of interorganizational cooperation. Corporate planning is most relevent, indeed indispensable, to the activities of business corporations which can measure their options and set their goals in quantitative terms. Similar techniques can be used by those public agencies which primarily operate according to commercial and technical criteria and to some extent by any agency which has specific and limited goals, preferably of a quantitative kind. Still, corporate planning has increasingly been recommend for multifunctional public bodies such as a city or county government. Robert Walker argued that the "planning function" in urban government must be related to all the functions locally performed and not just to the use and development of land.[9]

Walker's thesis is now widely accepted in Europe as well as the United States. Its attractions are obvious. It offers an apparent escape from the narrow and legalistic basis of physical planning as practiced locally, in favor of a broader concept of planning. Ideally this planning function would start with the general objectives of a local government for the welfare and development of the local community. It would build a data bank and information capacity for helping the local leadership to deal with (and if possible to anticipate) a diversity of policy problems. It would prepare a series of related plans covering budgeting, capital investment by public agencies, land use and development, and special plans for deprived areas and zones of major growth or renewal. These general plans would be linked with sectoral plans for transportation, housing, employment, and other key functions. The whole process would be implemented through cooperative teamwork between the chief officers and agency heads, guided and controlled by the political leadership serviced by a strong planning unit.

Corporate planning encounters tough problems of organizational cooperation which have both an internal and an external dimension. The internal requirement involves persuading the various departments and agencies of a city or county government to work together for common objectives. The difficulty in doing so, while formidable everywhere, is especially great where the structure of the city government is itself fragmented and includes a number of agencies having a legally distinct and quasiindependent status. This fragmentation of city government helps special interests to dominate particular policies.[10] An integrated city government should be more responsive to majority interests and concepts of community welfare.

The external problem of coordination concerns particularly the controls exercised by government departments over the various functions of a local government. These controls strengthen internal departmentalism, because they foster professional, financial, and policymaking linkages of a vertical kind. This problem is particularly marked in a European context because of the frequently high levels of direction and support provided by various central departments to local governments. One result is that the corporate plan cannot easily be squared with the various plans required to meet departmental specifications.

A theoretical answer would be for central government itself to make a corporate plan which would coordinate its various interventions. In practice the sheer scale of the central bureaucracy and the multiplicity of national policies seem to rub out this idea. Corporate planning has been recommended in England as a specific device for enabling a local government to combat central interventions with its own specific aims and priorities.[11]

A second major difficulty of corporate planning concerns the elucidation of its objectives. Theoretically these may be beamed at the general welfare of the local community. But in practice they will be concerned with the particular functions which a local government performs and especially with those which employ the most staff and consume the most resources. Corporate planning often uses techniques for resource allocation between competing ends. A danger is that its goals will be too narrowly defined by the weight of operating interests within the organization.

This discussion can be related to the types of organization discussed in this book. For a city, town planning becomes especially important when its government is undertaking large measures of physical development or renewal, but as the example of Stockholm suggests, effective planning turns more on the coordination of programs than on the land use plan itself, although the latter can be important. In periods of stringency corporate planning comes to the fore with a stress upon resource allocation among competing ends. Both types of planning tend to be too narrowly conceived and poorly related to each other.

Metro governments face similar problems in a different context. It was noted earlier that great stress has been laid upon metro's overall planning role. Still, this role has in practice been viewed primarily as the preparation of a broad physical plan, and metro governments such as London and Toronto have had little success with this objective. At the same time corporate planning by a metro government tends to become too dominated by the financial and other requirements of its principal operational tasks.

Regional planning organizations primarily produce framework plans which are sometimes more broadly conceived than the land use plans prepared by city or metro governments and which in favorable circumstances influence the plans of other governments. These bodies usually lack direct powers for implementing their plans.

Attempts have been made to integrate land use plans with broader (corporate) planning objectives. For example, the structure plans of metro and other counties in England are supposed to incorporate and reflect the "social and economic objectives" of the local government, but they have to comply with specifications of land use planning issued by the central ministry, and a land use plan is not a suitable vehicle for this task. Regional planning is more flexible in character because it usually does not produce statutory plans but relies upon guidelines and advice.

This discussion suggests that a broadly-based type of corporate planning, as discussed above, is in fact the best system for a city government. Statutory land use planning would be merely one branch of this activity, although physical planners would have an important contribution to make. The planning unit would need to be the *locus* of systematic planning and program coordination, not just a vehicle for staff assistance to the political leaders. It would need to have a diversified staff and to avoid the error of treating corporate planning as simply an exercise in accountancy and resource allocation.

At metro and regional levels a different type of planning is required. Neither corporate nor physical (framework) planning seems to provide the right answers. A concept of "strategic planning" is sometimes advanced to meet this situation, but it has rarely been adequately described. The following points may help to define the possible functions of a strategic planning authority (SPA):

1. The SPA would be concerned (as corporate planning is in principle) with general community objectives. The SPA would advance its goals, however, through the best organizational means available. Thus it would utilize smaller local governments, voluntary organizations, and other bodies for this purpose wherever practicable.
2. Its direct operating functions would be limited and related clearly to its goals. It would thereby gain a more objective and balanced

approach to coordinating the development plans and policies of other agencies. It would have strong powers to review (and then to accept, modify, or reject) the physical projects and financial plans produced by all major agencies within its region.

3. It would have powers to provide local governments and other bodies with financial and technical assistance. It would use these powers to help local communities that were poor or had special problems and to provide support facilities which might include certain specialized services requiring large-scale provision.

4. It would prepare a general regional plan and would have special power to intervene to aid in the plan's realization by means of advance land acquisition, industrial and economic promotion, the authority to undertake development projects by local agreement, and other measures.

5. Its exercise of financial powers would be critical. It should have general powers to approve and coordinate all major investments within its area and to operate an equlization scheme between local governments. It would be able to borrow for its own purposes and to operate a special fund for discretionary assistance. It would preferably draw upon an independent source of taxation.

6. The SPA would need to have an effective political base. Therefore it should presumably be directly elected, or if not it must at a minimum possess the full support of a higher level of government.

The kind of planning which an SPA should perform would be concerned equally with social, economic, and physical (environmental) goals. These should not be compartmentalized, as is often the case with existing planning procedures. All public policies are or should be beamed toward human welfare and happiness, and all interact. Economic policies have profound effects upon the volume and location of development and employment. Environmental policies provide good or bad conditions for economic enterprise and have effects upon the quality of life which fail to show up in economic indexes but are important for welfare. Social policies refer either to the special contributions of public social services or else more broadly to the presumed interests of communities as a whole (shared values).

Doubtless it would be utopian to envisage a full integration of all public policymaking, but some moves in this direction should be possible if policy issues can be effectively redefined, political support can be amassed for a new approach, and professional techniques can be synthesized. These requirements are the necessary basis for any successful administrative reform.

The last chapter, for example, illustrated the conflicts which often arise between economic and environmental policies. These conflicts derive from a differentiation of goals and political support: economic policies start with the national economy and work downward, resting upon a national constituency or the support of deprived regions, whereas environmental policies work from the buttom upward, resting upon a localized constituency which is widened gradually as the inter-dependencies of urbanization themselves grow. These differences become entrenched in organizational structures and are exaggerated by the techniques used to cope with apparently different phenomena. Thus for economic plans four years seems a long time because shifts in the economy are highly volatile, whereas physical plans look as much as twenty years ahead, a time period which corresponds to much slower rates of change in land use and development. Goals are influenced by the differentiation of time scales and techniques: economists think in terms of equilibrium or growth targets statistically tested, whereas environmental planners propose physical forms and designs whose effects can rarely be measured.

Closer examination shows the baleful effects of this differentiation of time scales and techniques. A more profitable distinction can be drawn between shorter-run stabilization measures (whether applied to the national economy or the local regulation of land use) and longer-term structural interventions (whether in the industrial system or the urban system). It is regional planning which needs especially to be concerned with long-term structural changes of this kind, which have to be related to the nature of the region's human, physical, and natural resources. Thus the regional plan prepared by an SPA would be not a statutory land use plan but a series of policies and standards which would be used to guide the development and conservation of regional resources so as to further the social values discussed earlier.

Methods of policy implementation, like the policies themselves, are often compartmentalized. The same basic techniques of economic incentives (taxes and subsidies), public regulation (the specification of standards), and direct public initiative (ownership and development) can apply in almost any policy situation. Yet traditional administrative procedures often fail to see these techniques as alternative or complementary ways of realizing the same objectives. For example, transportation policy is primarily set through economic incentives, but it could be strongly influenced by physical planning. Conversely, land use policies primarily utilize physical regulation, but they could employ economic incentives—for example, taxes on low-density development would be a way of reducing urban sprawl. There is also now a considerable American literature discussing the relative efficacy of economic and regulatory techniques for controlling pollution.

These points are no more than illustrations of the general role which a strategic planning authority might play. Whether or not a body of this kind is established, there is a need to consider the kind of positive planning which might be appropriate and possible under present-day conditions. The acceptability of powers and policies for this purpose will vary between societies, but the next section considers some of the possibilities, with special reference to the possible role of an SPA.

Methods of Positive Planning

1. *Land.* There are several reasons why land policy can be considered critical for urban planning. In the first place, the land market is a lottery where windfall gains and losses frequently occur beyond the control of landowners. Public investments in urban infrastructure, which represent a high proportion of total investment in the development process, bring about many of these gains and losses. Moreover, public planning of development shifts values between sites: the more tightly development is controlled, the larger is this shift of values and the higher also is the market value of sites where development is permitted. It is extremely costly for public authorities to pay adequate compensation for the adverse effects of planning unless they can recoup some at least of the increase in values which planning (and public investment generally) brings about. Consequently, either the land market becomes more of a lottery, or planning itself is negated.

Second, the scope for public participation is seriously harmed. There is official secrecy or delay over proposals with adverse effects ("planning blight"), and competition sometimes extends to corruption and bribery to secure the benefits of public decisions. Civic interest in community development is easily shouldered aside by these pressures.

Third, new public initiatives over land policy could improve planning without hurting the economy. Increases in land values which derive from the general growth of population and the economy have long been recognized in principle as an equitable source of revenue for helping to finance local public services and amenities. In a period of financial stringency, this is an important consideration in itself, if it can be realized. At the same time there need to no adverse effects upon commercial and industrial efficiency. For example, in the English new towns economic development does not seem to have been hindered by public ownership of the freeholds in land. It could be positively beneficial to divert to more directly productive purposes some of the increasing volume of savings which, partly because of inflation, are being invested in land. (For the United States it has been estimated that land comprises about 23 percent of all tangible assets or 13 percent if farmland and public land are excluded.)[12]

There are two possible forms of public action. One is to establish a workable system of compensation and betterment for coping with the adverse and profitable shifts of land values. The British history of land value legislation represents a one-sided treatment of this issue. The 1947 Planning Act largely denied compensation for restrictions placed upon a more intensive use of land. This provision has held and has made possible the extensive protection accorded to much rural land and the channeling of new development into specific locations. It has been much less useful in cities because local governments cannot reduce the intensity of land use without paying large compensation. The 1947 act also appropriated any increase in land value deriving from development permission, which amounted to a 100 percent betterment tax (although it did not cover increases in value which arise without any need for planning permission). This provision was repealed by a Conservative government in 1952. It was twice reenacted in a modified form by Labour governments in the 1960s and 1970s and was twice again repealed by the Conservatives.[13]

This brief history shows the political sensitivity of the land value issue. No reform can succeed if owners can reasonably anticipate its early repeal. The mismatch between compensation and betterment provisions in Britain is one obvious cause of inflated land values and risks or facts of corruption.

In the United States the attempts by some states to write down the value of the rural land for tax purposes so as to assist conservation have not worked too well and often involve taxpayers in a loss because they are not accompanied by any or a sufficient betterment levy. According to the more usual American approach, increasingly used elsewhere, the local government seeks a "planning gain" by requiring a developer to provide or pay for a number of local services and to deed land for public open space or other requirements. The principle of the "planning gain" appears equitable, although results vary greatly and turn upon a bargaining process open to political pressures and sometimes corruption. A more fundamental objection is that the main effect may be to pass on the costs to new residents in the form of higher prices for their homes rather than using the appreciation of land values to pay for the same services. The same effect is likely to occur with any levy imposed at the point of land development, its precise effects depending upon supply and demand in the land market. Still, general legislation should have more equitable and certain effects than bargaining with developers, and there are other (though admittedly difficult) methods of tackling compensation and betterment. Successful innovation here could reap great rewards.

The second possible policy is for public authorities to acquire substantial stocks of land as part of their planning operations.[14] Wisely done, betterment can now be recouped and used to secure the "planning gains" which must otherwise be bargained for with private developers or be foregone altogether. But the basic argument for public land banking is that it provides a key to the planning of development which is much more effective than regulatory powers. It is a form of positive town building illustrated by such European examples as the British new towns and Stockholm's satellite communities, whose essential basis was public land banking. It gives full recognition to the interests of communities in developing a safe, attractive, and convenient public domain free of countervailing pressures to maximize private profits in the use of land. It is consistent with the full participation of private enterprise in the development process itself.

Public land ownership can be exploited politically for sectional advantage and misused by organizations through lack of incentive to use land efficiently. These dangers are greatest where, as in Eastern Europe, there is a public land monopoly. They are reduced in Western countries by the political improbability of such a monopoly and by the incentives for public authorities to realize increases in value for their own purposes. Still, the benefits from public land ownership are clearly greatest when it is used as an instrument of coherent planning policies. The promotion of efficient economic production can then be combined with social and environmental aims, profits from the first activity being available to help finance the others.

The basic problem of public land banking is the financial one of acquiring sufficient land in advance and on suitable terms. Some cities all over the world have purchased land in advance of their needs as a matter of prudent foresight, and sometimes this land has proved vital to planning the city's subsequent growth. This policy has been assisted in a number of countries through the existence of powers to designate areas as liable to public acquisition on terms which seek to exclude the influence of the public project itself. This provision is most effective for isolated new towns but less so where escalating land values lap over into the protected zones. The main limitation is the financial inability or unwillingness of local governments to purchase sufficient land or of the national finance ministry to sanction and support such action.

A public land banking policy therefore needs to develop a considerable financial momentum and political acceptability. This situation was built up in Sweden, by the enterprise of cities like Stockholm and later by national legislation which required all local governments to establish a land bank sufficient for ten years' development requirements and which pegged public acquisition prices so as in principle to exclude development values. A strategic planning authority would be a very suitable body to undertake public land banking for agreed ends, either itself or through development agencies working under its control.

2. *Development.* If we review the many ways of planning new growth, the new town concept still has much to commend it. The concept is flexible enough to serve a variety of purposes. Emphasis has often been laid upon the creation of an efficiently functioning urban system through the concentration of facilities, the integration of homes and workplaces, transportation planning, conservation of land for certain purposes, and other measures. These physical concepts are linked with social aims, and latterly social values have got more attention. These include the design of towns which cater better to the needs of a variety of social and income groups and which at least assist, even if they cannot create, community life through such measures as creating a safe and attractive public domain.

The new town machinery of development, as it has functioned in Britain, has a number of advantages. The public commitment to build the town stimulates commercial and industrial development and produces economies of scale in some services. Public land assembly provides the basis for overall planning and can be made consistent with any desired partnership between public and private development. By using leasehold systems and reviewable rents, the public agency can secure increments in land value to be applied to the costs of town building and the provision of social and community facilities.

In the United States the new communities concept is often said to have failed, but this "failure" stemmed from an inadequate formulation of the basic aims. Most of the federally backed developments were private schemes which were sometimes poorly designed and weakly funded by the developers themselves. The projects were not related to a regional planning framework or to the development of public transportation facilities and other infrastructure. They did not incorporate a systematic process of public land banking, and their financing was not geared to the very long time and the techniques which a successful new town project requires. It is of course politically difficult to achieve any concerted or long-term deployment of public powers within the United States. Nonetheless a beneficial program once started would generate increasing support, and without it there can be no long-term development planning, since private enterprise will not absorb the risks of such ventures, unless they are conceived in narrow terms.[15] Public planning can reduce the risks through effective infrastructure planning and can introduce social policies which would not otherwise be viable.

Paradoxically the opposite situation in Britain of a financially viable new town program also generates political criticism. The present government (1980) is moving to sell off profitable new town assets in order to reduce the public sector debt, although paradoxically these assets represent one of the rare cases of successful public enterprise. The 1946 New Towns Act, following the example of pioneering garden cities such as Letchworth, envisaged that these assets should eventually be transferred to a local body for the benefit of the town. Since the initial capital was provided by the national treasury, it can alternatively be argued that some or all of the assets should help finance further projects.

Under future political conditions it seems likely that planning of new development will need to be broader in scope, but more limited and flexible over its use of public powers, than the British new town program has been. The initiative for designing and developing new communities may pass to a variety of agencies—to small local governments, cooperatives, and voluntary bodies, as well as private developers. This situation would accord with the growing pressures everywhere for more decentralization, more public participation, and above all more experimentation. The argument often heard (particularly in the United States) that planned developments will in any case absorb only a small proportion of total growth overlooks the value of testing and developing alternatives to present methods of urbanization.

A strategic authority could establish a framework for such activities by coordinating the pattern of development and by assembling and allocating land to the various community developers. It could adjust its land leases so as to ensure that sufficient provision was made for lower-income housing and other social needs. It could assist innovative projects concerned with transportation, energy saving, new community facilities, or the promotion of a greater degree of local self-sufficiency. In Britain the Town and Country Planning Association is trying to promote projects of this type as successors to the garden city concept.[16]

3. *Urban Renewal.* It has been said that the era of hard planning in cities involving big physical projects has given way to soft planning involving incremental change and adaptation of existing structures.[17] "Soft planning" implies a greater stress upon the maintenance of community structures, which may suggest the case for more conservation and rehabilitation. Still, this principle has to be made consistent with economic changes in the location of activities and with a substantial if more gradual volume of physical redevelopment.

The new tasks of city planning include the achievement of many small-scale transformations which are cumulatively substantial. For example, housing is needed for a variety of groups—such as skilled workers whose exodus has injured local industries, middle-class commuters wanting to return to the city, and low-income groups who are squeezed out by increasing numbers of owner occupiers. This situation requires many small projects to be built by a variety of agencies rather than big homogeneous projects. The housing, environmental, and employment aims can all be helped by a continuing fall in population, provided that this is gradual and balanced enough not to undermine community structures further.

A strategic planning authority would have a difficult task in old urban areas, but it could have a vital role. It should assemble land in key areas and upon a sufficient scale to reap the possible planning gains. It should promote big physical projects, for example, at transportation nodes. It can try to ensure that there is sufficient variety of housing through leasing land to cooperatives or nonprofit developers on suitable terms. It can assist the provision of small-scale industrial and craft workshops. It can provide cultural and recreational facilities. It can assist equalization of services through grants to smaller bodies and through its own transportation and other policies. It should avoid putting its resources into showcase developments which try to replicate the intensive urbanization of earlier days, even if these are for deprived areas like the London Docklands. It would preferably spread its aid among the many areas of deprivation.

4. *Transportation.* Planning here is becoming more sophisticated. On the one hand the high indirect costs of personal mobility are better perceived. This is a problem not only of mutually created congestion which figures prominently in transport economics but of the strong environmental impact of road traffic and airports. In addition the wide diffusion of facilities which accompanies extensive car ownership is high in energy costs and is injurious to all those dependent upon public or communal transport.

At the same time the considerable limitations of fixed rapid transport, except for long-distance travel and access to major centers, are also better appreciated. Subsidized suburban rail services primarily benefit relatively rich commuters. The same criticism has been leveled against an expensive, high technology rail system such as San Francisco's BART. Conversely, a number of urban plans have sought to make fixed rapid transport more viable through locating blocks of high-density housing near stations to be occupied by lower-income groups. To a point this arrangement is rational and occurs spontaneously, but it becomes unacceptable if it imposes unwanted housing conditions upon large numbers of people and thereby fosters a two-class community. Fortunately, with the decline of public housing programs, few such plans have been implemented.

Transportation policies can to some extent work through measures of traffic restraint and parking controls and by favoring modest systems such as buses. Beyond this point one encounters considerable variations in cultural and political values and in the physical structure of cities. Many American cities are laid out to meet the requirements of car travel in a way that could not apply to most European cities (and to some American ones). But in each case the city's structure can still be tilted so as to encourage more concentrated or more diffused facilities and so as to shift the relative advantages of private and public transport modes.

As suggested earlier, a planning authority should tackle these issues through a mixture of financial and physical measures. Thus if it is accepted that extensive personal mobility imposes high indirect costs, compensating taxes can be imposed which have some rough correspondence with the estimated damage. The effect will be to restrict the damage and to provide funds which could be used to compensate those harmfully affected.

Charges of this kind are often opposed on the grounds that they discriminate against poorer car owners or air travelers, but their main effect would be to raise the cost of transportation to everyone and to create less need for public transport subsidies. There seems no reason why transportation should be singled out for subsidization, as now certainly seems to be the case when its "externalities" are allowed for. Technology has already done more in this than in most other fields to stimulate development (often with large public subsidies for this purpose also).

Physical planning would aim to align transportation improvements with the development of new centers and subcenters. Within urban regions the fostering of major subcenters with scope for balanced access by both public and private transport could be used to establish greater equality of access and to encourage wider participation in communal activities. Such centers are especially needed in deprived inner areas where shopping and social facilities have declined together with the population.

At the same time, the location of key facilities such as a big airport needs to be appraised as much for its environmental and social effects as for its convenience to airport operators and users. The great importance of such an airport for regional development, and indeed for the balance of economic and social opportunities within an urban region, was noted in the last chapter. But to date there are very few examples (de Gaulle airport in Paris is one possible exception) of airports located according to broader regional goals.

5. *General.* The policies discussed in this section could be extended into other fields—for example, the planning of employment. Employment issues have not been discussed further because of the crucial importance of national and international economic policies which would widen the analysis still more. Nonetheless, regional planning for employment

remains highly important within this broader framework. It is necessary, for example, to try to plan the pattern of development so as to assist the growth of those industries which have potential growth prospects in a particular locality. A structural approach to economic development at the regional level can help at least to reduce the mutual frustrations produced by interregional compettiton for whatever mobile industry is available.

It may be objected that this section has strayed well beyond the capacities of any urban planning authority, however broadly based, into questions of national legislation and policies. This is certainly true. The basic powers would have to be nationally determined and in some cases controlled by national agencies. Still, it is a possible assumption that considerable powers may devolve upon some type of strategic planning authority whose character will be further considered in the next section. If this is not so, the same policy issues still arise, although the policies themselves would be applied in a less integrated manner. Conversely, of course, whatever new organizations came into existence, there can be no certain knowlege of the policies that they will follow. That remains a question of political choice.

Political and Organizational Choices

Early in this book the urban region was described as a political and organizational crossroads. From a comparative perspective one notes a multitude of public agencies but few clear or coherent frameworks for coping with urbanization issues. In those cases where a suitable agency does exist, it seems to do so by the happenstance of history and geography. Without supposing there to be any easy solutions, it is time to consider what system of government is most likely to achieve effective planning and performance.

The value of the traditional form of big city government ought first to be recognized. It provides a unification of powers in a single government within a reasonably compact area. It did and to some extent still does correspond to a discernible geographic and political community. Civic loyalties and passions, and civic pride, have always been more intense than the interests aroused by other types of local government. The complications of a two-tiered local government system, with its diffusion of political interest and its difficulties of functional cooperation, can largely be avoided through a system of strong city government. Effective city government can also be combined with the existence of both local and regional units, provided they do not undermine its basic importance.

For example, elected local neighborhood councils can be established to express the rising pressures for public participation at this level. They would have few or no powers beyond a statutory right to consultation in the decisions of the city government. Their existence would also make large city governments more acceptable politically. City government could also be combined with a system of regional planning and coordination for discharging some of the "strategic functions" discussed earlier. Provided that this regional body was primarily an offshoot of central government, or a partnership arrangement between central and local government, it need not conflict with a strong role for city government, although elective regional institutions with strong powers would diminish the city's role.

As the government framework widens, the planning of urbanization becomes theoretically and functionally more rational but tends to lose its political base and to become entangled with other policy issues. It seems that popular identification of a common metropolitan existence and set of interests declines steadily with distance from the main center, although this may be due to the political separatism of suburbanites rather than to their failure to recognize the existence of common problems. Few people, however, appear to recognize their membership of an entity called an urban or city region or to appreciate its functional importance except for transportation—and popular interest in that subject grows spottier as one moves outward. The influence of other regional interests of an economic or ethnic character will in some circumstances be perceived much more strongly.

The metro governments discussed in chapter 3 have at least some potential for achieving a viable political and functional base that would be rooted specifically in the shared problems of urbanization. But this potential is much weakened by the actual organizational circumstances in which they have been required to operate. They must in many cases share powers with large local governments which are not sufficiently differentiated from the metro in terms of their physical size and which have as strong or stronger a political and organizational base—although at each level this base is weakened by the inadequate differentiation of roles. In terms of organization theory, the span of control is too narrow for the performance of a strategic planning function. At the same time, central governments have generally not invested metro governments with the powers necessary for an effective strategic role or have not backed up their efforts by prompt arbitration of intergovernmental disputes.

The problems of metros have been further increased by the circumstance that their arrival coincided with a period of rapid population and economic decline in many urban areas and with a series of hasty government interventions in urban policies. In confronting these problems metros lacked the concentrated set of powers possessed by a traditional city government but often lacked also the compensating advantage of covering areas of growth as well as decline. In these circumstances it is easy to appreciate the views of those, like the first chairman of Metro Toronto, who have concluded that a unified city government would after all be a preferable arrangement. The issue of big city government is not yet buried in Toronto or elsewhere, and the thesis can still be rationally argued. Despite all these drawbacks the metro experiments have achieved some worthwhile results and may be capable of improvement into a more viable form.

It is now time to revert to the concept of a strategic planning function. This concept was elaborated on a test basis in order to give more precision to the idea that some body should have a degree of overall responsibility for the management of urban change and growth. It was suggested that the keys to strategic planning resided in (a) the effective coordination of many public agencies involved in urban development; (b) selective aid and support to smaller local governments and to voluntary and other bodies; (c) powers for selective intervention in the functioning of urban systems. These actions would be based upon general objectives for the welfare of the people of the region, would require an integration of physical and economic planning, and would utilize financial as well as physical controls and interventions.

These strategic planning functions are possessed in varying degrees by a number of the government bodies discussed in this book. They can be clearly discerned in the roles of such diverse organizations as the Région d'Ile-de-France, the Stockholm county council, and the Twin Cities metropolitan council. But in what form could functions of this type be generalized?

The most obvious answer would be a form of elective regionalism. As was suggested earlier, the choice of regions could not in practice be based closely upon the city region concept. This concept has contributed very significantly to the debate on local government reform and regionalism, as chapter 3 showed. However, it does not itself provide a fully adequate basis for regionalism. The varying size and influence of big cities would itself make for an unbalanced set of regions, but in addition economic and ethnic or cultural factors could not and should not be excluded from the design of a regional system. Still, it need not matter too much if a region sometimes covered more than one urban system, provided that regional boundaries were reasonably related to the facts and prospects of urbanization. Undoubtedly urban issues would form a major part of the regional body's agenda.

Direct election of the regional body would, as suggested earlier, provide the vital base for the exercise of financial powers of taxation and resource allocation. The regional body would be able to make an economic and physical plan for its area, and it would be logically placed (if the legal powers existed) to exercise the selective interventions in land assembly and development policies discussed in the last section. It would be a suitable coordinator of transportation policies. It would have both the strength and the detachment to assist local governments and voluntary bodies in the ways described, to provide specialized services for local government generally, and to operate a plan of financial equalization. It could best undertake some of these tasks—for example, land assembly or new towns—through the medium of public corporations appointed by itself. Such activities as public transport could be controlled in the same way, and for "independent" public corporations there would need to be the strong review powers mentioned earlier. Of course one cannot know what political choices an elected regional body would actually make but only show its potential capacities.

Tempting as this vision of a new regionalism may be, there must be serious political doubts about its realism. There doubts do not center upon the well-worn question of whether a meaningful sense of community exists at the regional level. It has been agreed already that this sense is weakly present within the context of the urban region. The strength of ethnic regionalism is hardly helpful because it is so unevenly spread and sometimes has extreme objectives. It is possible to underestimate the extent of cultural regionalism which still exists and seems to be reviving. But the main point is that the existence of significant common problems will be enough to generate an effective regional constituency once appropriate instituions exist. The existence of these problems is demonstrated by the large number of regional bodies which everywhere exist, by the many partial attempts at regional planning, and by the nature of modern urbanization itself. The difficulty is to establish regional institutions that are genuinely capable of tackling these problems.

The difficulties over establishing such institutions differ between unitary and federal states. In the former cases political and bureaucratic power has become centralized and resistant to regional devolution except where ethnic separatism has to be appeased. Even the creation of elected regional bodies might not establish effective decentralization, if national political parties and central departments kept a strong grip on their operations. In federations state governments already represent strong regional institutions of a certain type, but their constitutions, areas, and powers are poorly suited to the requirements of regional planning.

Effective regional planning does not require a constitutional division of sovereignties, such as exists formally in federations, nor yet a formal devolution of national legislative powers and a replication of national executive machinery, such as is sometimes represented as being a desirable reform within unitary states. These devices put their emphasis upon generalized legislation and policymaking which produces a replication of the national government's functions rather than the creation of more flexible systems of planning, oversight, intervention, and support. A regional planning agency need not aspire to constitutional or even legislative independence from the center, but it would need a sufficiently independent political base to develop its own policies and make its own decisions within the framework of the formal powers granted it.

Elective regional bodies of this kind would make the metro concept redundant because they would absorb on a broader basis the strategic planning function allocated to metro, and because the multiplication of tiers of government spells political and organizational fragmentation and ineffectiveness. The creation of effective regional governments would leave the road clear for the adoption of a "unitary" system of local government—or if one looks at it differently, of a combined regional-cum-local system. This situation would be consistent with a strong role for the basic tier of local governments operating within the framework of strategic planning exercised at the regional level. Controversy would still remain about the desirable size of local units and in particular of the governments of large cities. A regional system would combine much better than does a metro system with the rationalization of local government into larger and more homogeneous units which has now occurred in many urban areas through national legislation in a number of countries. In this situation big city governments could be regarded as unnecessary, given the upward shift of some key functions. But big cities would certainly be less anomalous within a regional context than within a metro context.

The only alternative to fully elective regionalism would be a strengthening of the joint planning machinery, both between government departments and between central and local government, which already exists at this level. This coordinative machinery performs important tasks where it has been fully developed because of the number of organizational interests covered and the springboard which it sometimes provides for a relatively "objective" approach to regional planning. But the political weakness of this machinery severely restricts, as was said before, the kind of planning that can be done. It is possible to devise various halfway houses between purely administrative and fully elective forms of regionalism, as is the case with the French regional institutions. But there remains an incompatability between regional planning functioning primarily as an offshoot of central governments, and regional planning as it would be executed by a politically independent body. French regionalism primarily corresponds to the former activity. This activity could be strengthened only through its sponsorship by a stronger central agency and through a better integration of government departments. Difficult as this may be, it is the only way forward if power is strongly centralized. Independent regional bodies could count less upon the cooperation of central departments and would need to take over some central functions if they were to be effective.

It is, of course, the function of central legislatures and governments to determine the structure and functions of lesser authorities. In federations, unless or until the constitution is changed, this task devolves primarily upon state governments. It might be very desirable that the constitution should be changed, but that issue transcends the scope of this book. As things stand, a state government normally has the constitutional responsibility for local government and is much more logically placed to settle the framework of urban government and planning than a federal government is. Federal efforts to bypass states and to establish a more direct role in urban planning have not been effective. They have complicated more than they have improved the urban system of management. Thus as things stand the more profitable course for federal governments is to concentrate upon improving the role of the states primarily through the use of financial incentives. This is a complex and important task.

Generally speaking, central and state governments have not faced up well to their responsibilities. There is much rhetoric in the modern world about the value of decentralization, but the concept is rarely investigated rigorously. The principles for desirable forms of decentralization need first to be laid down and then implemented through regular and systematic reviews of the structure and powers of local government systems. These reviews should also comprehend the regional function of government departments and the role of big public corporations. Instead of regular reviews the usual practice is intermittent and ad hoc reforms which are influenced by current political pressures and rarely come to grips with the basic issues. The same general framework of government administration persists irrespective of these occasional reforms, and the tendency to centralization stays unaltered. This has been a main reason for the difficulties of metro governments. The situation probably will not change until a political movement develops which genuinely wants some decentralization of effective power.

To summarize, the most desirable development in principle would be the creation of directly elected regional authorities performing a strategic planning role. This development would build upon the experiments with metro governments (where such exist) through converting the metros into larger units possessing a different range of powers, a

shift which would also facilitate cooperation between the elected regional bodies and smaller local governments. The new regional bodies
would take over some powers now exercised by central or state governments, and they would require from these governments a clear grant of
the necessary authority to undertake successful strategic planning. If,
however, the governmental and political system must be judged too
centralized for the reform to be practicable, central or state government
will itself need to operate (in cooperation with local governments) a
system of strategic planning at the regional level and to strengthen its
organization and consultative machinery for this purpose. This overhaul
should be accompanied by a full review of local government systems,
which should include reconsideration of the respective merits of metro
systems and big city governments, as well as possible changes for
increasing effectiveness and acceptability—for example, by extending
city boundaries but combating "remoteness" through a formal system of
neighborhood councils. The political effects of such reforms would be
complex. It is received wisdom that the way to enhance the influence of
general over special interests is through an appeal to broader constituencies and to more integrated governmental systems. Thereby the
majoritarian principle gets greater leverage. On the whole this assumption seems correct, but how it works out depends upon who constitutes
a majority and how this majority sees its interests.

City governments often possess a constituency where the majority is
relatively underprivileged. This situation provided a powerful impetus for
the welfare goals pursued by many European cities during the years
after World War II. In American cities this situation was for long less
apparent because of the powerful grip of business interests and the
financial constraints under which cities operated. More recently, however, the election of black mayors in a number of American cities has
signaled the emergence of an underprivileged majority in search of
radical solutions to the problems of urban ghettoes. The solutions that
can be found are still constrained, however, by the financial and economic system which sometimes produces the prospect or fact of civic
bankruptcy.

A switch to metro government changes the constituency. That is why
metro schemes are now increasingly feared as a political trap by black
civic leaders in the United States and why, conversely, they may become more popular among white suburbanites. This opposition mirrors
within a different policy context the kind of fierce opposition to the
London government reform expressed by the London Labour party. In
practice metro authorities in London and in England have a balanced
constituency and are politically volatile. To date the effect has been
frequent political turnovers and rapid policy changes which have prej-

udiced or precluded any consistent approach to the tasks of strategic planning. It is not necessary for political volatility to negate institutional effectiveness, but this result is likely to occur when the institutional role itself is obscure, controversial, and weakly established.

An appeal to still broader regional constituencies would have different effects. Here differentiation between the politics of deprived and prosperous regions would be likely to result. Radicalism in the former constituencies would be limited, however, by the weakness of their economic base.

In the end the main question is not whether an appeal to broader constituencies produces more radical or more conservative policies. It can of course do either. The question rather is whether an effective majority may come to see a more positive form of planning as desirable. The assumption in this chapter has been that some shift in the scope and powers of collective decision making would help societies to emerge from the economic and social deadlocks in which they are now gripped. The assumption may of course be unacceptable. But if it proved true, political choice would come to be exercised within a changed context of the governmental role and powers. This shift, once accomplished, would generate political effects which would give new meanings to "conservative" or "radical."

Organizational systems themselves cannot be separated from the powers they possess and have to be designed with some view of desirable powers and policies in view. Whether they will work in the predicated way cannot be known. The organizational system is too complex and there are too many political variables. But the planning of urbanization has been none too successful to date, and it is reasonable to suggest that new initiatives in policy and organization are both needed.

Notes

Chapter 1

1. Colin Clark, *Population Growth and Land Use* (London: Macmillan, 1967), provides a full analysis of these trends.

2. The number of millionaire agglomerations in the world increased from 16 in 1900 to 68 in 1950, and 152 in 1970; 399 are predicted for the year 2000. For the more developed regions, the figures are 14, 45, 81, and 140. (United Nations data extracted from world housing survey, 1974)

3. Brian J. L. Berry, ed., *Urbanization and Counterurbanization* (Beverly Hills, Calif.: Sage Publications, 1976).

4. M. M. Webber et al., *Explorations into Urban Structure* (London: Oxford University Press, 1964).

5. H. G. Wells, *Anticipations: The Reaction of Mechanical Progress on Human Life and Thought* (1901; reprint ed., London: Harper & Row, 1962).

6. I use the term "urban region" rather than "city region," since the system may be polynucleated either because there exist several central cities which have grown into or collided with each other (as reflected in the British word "conurbation") or because several major secondary centers have been subsequently established. The concept of the urban region as a basis for local government is discussed in chapter 3.

7. For a good review see C. E. Lindblom, *Politics and Markets* (New York: Basic Books, 1977).

8. E. C. Banfield, *The Unheavenly City* (Boston: Little, Brown, 1968).

9. For a fuller analysis see Alan A. Altshuler, *The City Planning Process: A Political Analysis* (Ithaca, N.Y.: Cornell University Press, 1965).

10. Herbert Gans, *People and Plans* (New York: Basic Books, 1968).

11. See in particular David Harvey, *Social Justice and the City* (London: Edward Arnold, 1973), and H. Castells, *The Urban Question* (London: Edward Arnold, 1977).

12. Sir Geoffrey Vickers, *The Art of Judgement* (London: Chapman and Hall, 1975).

13. C. E. Lindblom, *The Policy Making Process* (Englewood Cliffs, N.J.: Prentice-Hall, 1968).

14. D. A. Rondinelli, *Urban and Regional Development Planning* (Ithaca, N.Y.: Cornell University Press, 1975), and A. J. Catanese, *Planners and Local Politics: Impossible Dreams* (Beverly Hills, Calif.: Sage Publications, 1974).

15. For more about the postwar consensus, see Peter Self, *Cities in Flood*, 2nd ed. (London: Faber & Faber, 1961). For party politics see D. Mackay and A. Cox, *The Politics of Urban Change* (London: Croom Helm, 1979).

16. John Delafons, *Land Use Controls in the United States* (Cambridge, Mass.: Harvard University Press, 1970).

17. J. B. Cullingworth, *Town and Country Planning in Britain* (London: George Allen & Unwin, 1974).

18. David Donnison, *The Government of Housing* (London: Penguin, 1967).

19. Charles R. Adrian, "Suburbia and the Folklore of Metropology," *Public Administration Review* 21, no. 2 (Summer 1961): 148–53.

20. W. S. Sayre and H. Kaufman, *Governing New York City* (New York: Russell Sage Foundation, 1960).

21. "Gotham in the Air Age," in *Public Administration and Policy Development: A Case Book*, ed. Harold Stein (New York: Harcourt, Brace, 1952), pp. 143–97.

22. Hugh Stretton, *Ideas for Australian Cities* (Melbourne: Georgian House, 1970), chaps. 6 and 7.

23. J. A. Clapp, *New Towns and Urban Policy* (New York: Dunellen, 1971), pp. 186–87.

Chapter 2

1. Robert C. Wood, *1,400 Governments* (Cambridge, Mass.: Harvard University Press, 1964).

2. Winston Crouch, "Los Angeles," in *Great Cities of the World*, ed. W. A. Robson and D. E. Regan (London: George Allen & Unwin, 1972).

3. Paul Peterson, *City Limits* (Chicago: University of Chicago Press, 1981).

4. L. J. Sharpe, ed., *The Fiscal Crisis in West European Local Government: Myths and Realities* (London: Sage Publications, 1980).

5. E. C. Banfield, *Political Influence* (Glencoe, Ill.: Free Press, 1961).

6. J. L. Pressman, *Federal Programs and City Politics* (Berkeley: University of California Press, 1975).

7. For information about New Haven, see R. A. Dahl, *Who Governs? Democracy and Power in an American City* (New Haven: Yale University Press, 1961). About Newark see Howard Kaplan, "Urban Renewal in Newark," in *Urban Renewal: The Record and the Controversey*, ed. J. A. Wilson (Cambridge, Mass.: M.I.T. Press, 1966), pp. 233–58. For the Chicago housing plan see M. Meyerson and E. Banfield, *Politics, Planning, and the Public Interest* (Glencoe, Ill.: Free Press, 1964).

8. S. Elkin, *Politics and Land Use Planning: The London Experience* (London: Cambridge University Press, 1974).

9. T. J. Anton, *Governing Greater Stockholm* (Berkeley: University of California Press, 1975).

10. Altshuler, *City Planning Process*, chaps. 1–4.

11. Sayre and Kaufman, *Governing New York City*, pp. 372–80.

12. F. F. Rabinovitz, *City Politics and Planning* (New York: Atherton Press, 1969).

13. Hans Wohlin, "Stockholm's Experience of Decentralized Concentration" (Stockholm: Department of Planning, 1975), and "Information on Housing Renewal in Stockholm" (Stockholm: Real Estate Department, 1978).

14. P. J. Dunleavy, *The Politics of Mass Housing in Britain* (London: Oxford University Press, 1981).

15. J. B. Cullingworth, *Environmental Planning*, vol 3. *New Towns Policy* (London: HMSO, 1979).

16. Self, *Cities in Flood*, chap. 3, and Cullingworth, *Environmental Planning*, chap. 9.

17. Kell Astrom, *City Planning in Sweden* (Stockholm: Swedish Institute, n.d.).

18. Anton, *Governing Greater Stockholm*, p. 73.

19. See chapter 3 below.

20. David Pass, *Vällingby and Farsta—From Idea to Reality: The New Community Development in Stockholm* (Cambridge, Mass.: M.I.T. Press, 1973).

21. Dunleavy, *Politics of Mass Housing in Britain*, gives a review of causes.

22. David Popenoe, *The Suburban Environment: Sweden and the United States* (Chicago: University of Chicago Press, 1977). See also chapter 5 below.

23. For interregional policies affecting big cities, see chapter 4.

24. Department of Housing and Urban Development, *The President's National Urban Policy Report* (Washington, D.C.: U.S. Government Printing Office, 1978).

25. C. G. Bentham and M. J. Moseley, "Socio-economic Change and Disparities within the Paris Agglomeration: Does Paris Have an 'Inner City Problem'?" *Regional Studies* 14, no. 1: 55–70.

26. See D. Donnison and D. Eversley, eds., *London: Urban Patterns, Problems, and Policies* (London: Heinemann, 1973).

27. For a general review see John P. Crecine, ed., *Financing the Metropolis* (Beverly Hills, Calif.: Sage Publications, 1970).

28. J. Q. Wilson, ed., *Urban Renewal: The Record and the Controversy* (Cambridge, Mass.: M.I.T. Press, 1966). See also M. Anderson, *The Federal Bulldozer* (Cambridge, Mass.: M.I.T. Press, 1964).

29. D. P. Moynihan, *Maximum Feasible Misunderstanding* (New York: Free Press, 1969).

30. B. J. Frieden and Marshall Kaplan, *The Politics of Neglect* (Cambridge, Mass.: M.I.T. Press, 1975).

31. S. H. Beer, "Political Overload and Federalism," *Polity* 10, no. 1 (Fall 1977): 5–17. For CDBG see Brookings Institution report by Richard P. Nathan et al., "Block Grants for Community Development" (Washington, D.C.: Department of Housing and Urban Development, 1977).

32. John Edwards and Richard Batley, *The Politics of Positive Discrimination: An Evaluation of the Urban Programme, 1967–77* (London: Tavistock Publications, 1978).

33. See chapter 5 below.

34. R. D. Bingham, *Public Housing and Urban Renewal* (New York: Praeger, 1975), p. 14.

35. Jane Jacobs, *The Life and Death of Great American Cities* (London: Penguin, 1972).

36. S. E. Rasmussen, *London, the Unique City* (Cambridge, Mass.: M.I.T. Press, 1967).

Chapter 3

1. Strictly, the term "metro scheme" should refer to the capital region or metropolis, but it has now passed into general usage for big urban areas.

2. *Report of the Royal Commission on Local Government in England,* vol. 1, cmnd. 4040. (London: HMSO, 1969): pp. 70–73.

3. The classic statement of this thoery is by Charles M. Tiebout in "A Pure Theory of Local Expenditure," *Journal of Political Economy* 64, no. 5 (1956): 416–24. It assumes effective individual mobility and the absence of social or political discrimination.

4. Brian J. L. Berry, *The Human Consequences of Urbanization* (London: Macmillan, 1973).

5. Oliver P. Williams, *Metropolitan Political Analysis* (New York: Free Press, 1971), chap. 7.

6. Dorothy Nelkin, *Jetport* (New Brunswick, N.J.: Transaction Books, 1974).

7. Howard M. Hallman, *Small and Large Together: Governing the Metropolis* (Beverly Hills, Calif.: Sage Publications, 1977).

8. *Report of the Royal Commission on Local Government in Greater London,* cmnd. 1164 (London: HMSO, 1960).

9. *Report of the Royal Commission on Local Government in England,* pp. 95–108.

10. Charles Warren, "Regional Reform," in *The Regionalist Papers,* ed. Kent Mathewson (Southfield, Mich.: Metropolitan Fund, 1978), pp. 239–63.

11. See further, Peter Self, "Economic Ideas and Government Operations," *Political Studies* 23 (1975): 2–3.

12. Gerald Rhodes, ed., *The New Government of London, the First Five Years* (London: Weidenfeld & Nicolson, 1972).

13. For further discussion and references, see chapter 5.

14. For the history of Toronto see Albert Rose, *Governing Metropolitan Toronto* (Berkeley: University of California Press, 1972); Harold Kaplan, *Urban Political Systems: A Functional Analysis of Metro Toronto* (New York: Columbia University Press, 1967); Frank Smallwood, *Metro Toronto—A Decade Later* (Toronto: Bureau of Municipal Research, 1963); Eric Hardy, "Toronto and Montreal," in *Great Cities of the World,* ed. W. A. Robson and D. E. Regan (London: George Allen & Unwin, 1972); *Report of the Royal Commission on Metropolitan Toronto,* 2 vols. (Government of Ontario, 1977). See also the background reports of the royal commission, especially *The Planning Process in Metropolitan Toronto, Transport*

158

Notes to Pages 67–76

Organization in Metropolitan Toronto, The Electoral System for Metropolitan Toronto, A Financial Profile of Metropolitan Toronto (Government of Ontario, 1975).

15. For origins of London reform, see *Report of the Royal Commission on Local Government in Greater London.* For history and evaluations see Frank Smallwood, *Greater London: The Politics of Metropolitan Reform* (New York: Bobbs-Merrill, 1965); Donald L. Foley, *Governing the London Region* (Berkeley: University of California Press, 1972); Gerald Rhodes, *The Government of London: The Struggle for Reform* (London: Weidenfeld & Nicolson, 1972); and Rhodes, *New Government of London.* The last two books are among the publications of the Greater London Group at the London School of Economics (late chairman, Prof. W. A. Robson), which played an active part in the original reform and has monitored progress since in a series of books and papers.

16. The history of the Stockholm reform is fully analyzed in Anton, *Governing Greater Stockholm.*

17. See *The Planning Process in Metropolitan Toronto,* and Rose, *Governing Metropolitan Toronto.*

18. Peter Self, *Metropolitan Planning: The Planning System of Greater London,* Greater London paper no. 14 (London: London School of Economics, 1971).

19. Department of the Environment, *Report of the Panel of Inquiry,* 2 vols (London: HMSO, 1972). The inquiry itself lasted 237 days and considered 28,207 objections and mountains of written as well as verbal evidence.

20. Compare the rather narrow *Report of Studies* which accompanied the GLDP (Greater London Council, 1969) with the earlier base studies of the *New York Metropolitan Region Studies,* 9 vols. (Cambridge, Mass.: Harvard University, Press, 1960).

21. C. F. Ahlberg, "Planning the Stockholm Region" (1975); Hans Wohlin, "The Planning of Stockholm" (1978) and "Framework for Urban Development in Sweden" (1978); and other information available from the Swedish Institute and city of Stockholm.

22. M. F. Collins and T. M. Pharoah, *Transport Organizations in a Great City* (London: George Allen & Unwin, 1974); D. Hart, *Strategic Planning in London: The Rise and Fall of the Primary Road Network* (Oxford: Pergamon, 1976); Royal Commission, *Transport Organization in Metropolitan Toronto;* Hardy, "Toronto and Montreal."

23. Department of the Environment, *Report of the Panel of Inquiry.*

24. J. Michael Thomson, *Great Cities and Their Traffic* (London: Penguin, 1978), pp. 269–87.

25. Self, *Metropolitan Planning,* chap. 5, and J. M. Thomson, *Motorways in London* (London: Duckworth, 1969).

26. J. Kramer and K. Young, *Strategy and Conflict in Metropolitan Housing* (London: Heinemann, 1978). The authors adopt an American-style view of the problem of "opening up the suburbs" which overlooks the large impact of overspill housing in Britain.

27. See *A Financial Profile of Metropolitan Toronto* and for London boroughs the annual general and rating statistics of the Chartered Institute of Public Finance and Accountancy. Also see R. Kirwan, "The Contribution of Public Expenditure

and Finance to the Problems of Inner London," in *London: Urban Patterns, Problems and Policies,* ed. D. Donnison and D. Eversley (London: Heinemann, 1973).

28. See Derek Senior, ed., *The Regional City* (London: Longmans Green, 1966) for a general account of the case. For a later collection of views, see T. Hancock, ed., *Growth and Change in the Future City Region* (London: Leonard Hill, 1976).

29. Ministry of Housing and Local Government, *The Future of Development Plans,* Report of the Planning Advisory Group (London: HMSO, 1965).

30. *Report of Royal Commission on Local Government in England.* Senior's dissenting memorandum was published as vol. 2, cmnd. 4040–1, of the report (London: HMSO, 1969).

31. Peter G. Richards, *The Reformed Local Government System* (London: George Allen & Unwin, 1975).

32. *Report of the Royal Commission on Local Government in Scotland,* cmnd. 4150 (Edinburgh: HMSO, 1969). See also Foley, *Governing the London Region,* chap. 7.

33. A. Bours, "The Netherlands: Reorganization of Local Government" (Amsterdam: Institute of Public Administration, n.d.).

34. J. C. Thoenig, "Local Government Institutions and the Contemporary Evolution of French Society," in *Local Government in Britain and France,* ed. J. Lagroye and V. Wright (London: George Allen & Unwin, 1979).

35. Peter Hall, *The World Cities* (London: Weidenfeld & Nicolson, 1977), pp. 138–49.

36. John C. Bollens and Henry J. Schmandt, *The Metropolis* (New York: Harper & Row, 1970), chap. 12; John J. Harrigan, *Political Change in the Metropolis* (Boston, Mass.: Little, Brown, 1976), chaps. 6–8.

37. Bollens and Schmandt, *Metropolis,* chap. 13; Crouch, "Los Angeles," in *Great Cities,* pp. 575–603.

38. See Mathewson, *Regionalist Papers,* and Melvin B. Mogulof, *Governing Metropolitan Areas: A Critical Review of Councils of Governments and the Federal Role* (Washington, D.C.: Urban Institute, 1971).

39. Victor Jones, "San Francisco Bay Area Regionalism," in Mathewson, *Regionalist Papers,* pp. 133–60.

40. See Ted Kolderie, "Regionalism in the Twin Cities of Minnesota," in Mathewson, *Regionalist Papers,* pp. 26–47.

41. Robin Hambleton, *Policy Planning and Local Government* (London: Hutchinson, 1978).

42. P. H. Wickern, ed., *The Development of Urban Government in the Winnipeg Area* (Province of Manitoba: Department of Urban Affairs, n.d.).

Chapter 4

1. *Report of the Royal Commission on the Distribution of Industrial Population,* cmnd. 6153 (London: HMSO, 1940).

2. For histories of British and French policies, and comparisons between

them, see Lloyd Rodwin, *Nations and Cities* (Boston: Houghton Mifflin, 1970), chaps. 5 and 6; James Sundquist, *Dispersing Population* (Washington, D.C.: Brookings Institution, 1975), chaps. 2 and 3; and Hall, *World Cities*, chaps. 2 and 3.

3. *Second Report on Physical Planning in the Netherlands* (The Hague: Government Printing Office, 1966); Hall, *World Cities*, chap. 4 (Netherlands); Sundquist, *Dispersing Population*, chaps. 5 and 6 (Netherlands, Sweden).

4. Hall, *World Cities*, chap. 6 (Moscow). The largest Russian cities have nonetheless persistently grown much faster than planned as a result of industrial growth. Hugh Stretton, *Urban Planning in Rich and Poor Countries* (Oxford: Oxford University Press, 1978), pp. 194–95.

5. The Nixon quotation is from the executive order creating the Council for Urban Affairs, 1969. Quoted in Rodwin, *Nations and Cities*, p. 263.

6. U.S. Commission on Population Growth and the American Future, *Population and the American Future* (Washington, D.C.: U.S. Government Printing Office, 1972).

7. For growth point concepts in France, see N. M. Hansen, *French Regional Planning* (Bloomington: Indiana University Press, 1968), chap. 5, and J. R. Boudeville, *Regional Economic Planning* (Edinburgh: Edinburgh University Press, 1966).

8. J. Hayward and M. Watson, eds., *Planning, Politics, and Public Policy* (Cambridge: Cambridge University Press, 1975).

9. P. Hall, *Theory and Practice of Regional Planning* (London: Pemberton Books, 1970).

10. Self, *Cities in Flood*, chap. 6.

11. John Glasson, *An Introduction to Regional Planning* (London: Hutchison, 1974), pp. 214–83. Glasson (pp. 333–37) gives a useful list of sixty-eight major regional or subregional planning studies prepared in the United Kingdom mainly since 1965. These show the influence of the planning councils. Wales has the least (three), Scotland (twelve), and the South-East (eight) the most.

12. Pierre Grémion and Jean-Pierre Worms, "The French Regional Planning Experiments," in Hayward and Watson, *Planning, Politics*, pp. 217–37, and Hansen, *French Regional Planning*. DATAR has a special fund, equal to about 1 percent of the government's capital budget, to trigger developments. See G. Ross and S. Cohen, *The Politics of French Regional Planning* (Baltimore: Johns Hopkins University Center for Metropolitan Planning and Research, 1973).

13. V. Wright and H. Machin, "The French Regional Reforms of July 1972: A Case of Disguised Centralization," in *Policy and Politics* 3, no. 3 (1975): 3–28, and V. Wright, "Regionalization under the French Fifth Republic, the Triumph of the Functional Approach," in L. J. Sharpe, ed., *Decentralist Trends in Western Europe* (Beverly Hills, Calif.: Sage Publications, 1979).

14. For the métropoles d'équilibres, see Rodwin, *Nations and Cities*, pp. 193–201; Sundquist, *Dispersing Population*, pp. 111–32; Glasson, *Introduction to Regional Planning*, pp. 284–99; Hansen, *French Regional Planning*.

15. C. Sorbet, "Control of Urban Development in France," in *Local Government in Britain and France*, ed. Lagroye and Wright, pp. 150–65.

16. Rodwin, *Nations and Cities*, pp. 229–33.

17. Martha Derthick, *Between State and Nation* (Washington, D.C.: Brookings Institution, 1974), chaps. 4 and 5 and appendix.

18. Hugh Evans and Lloyd Rodwin, "The New Towns Program and Why It Failed," *Public Interest,* no. 56 (Summer 1979), pp. 90–107, and interviews with HUD officials.

19. Sundquist, *Dispersing Population,* pp. 128–32 (France) and pp. 65–66 (England).

20. M. Frost and N. Spence, "A More Selective Regional Policy?" *Town and Country Planning* 49, no. 8 (Sept. 1980): 252–55.

21. U.S. Department of Housing and Urban Development, *The President's National Urban Policy Report* (Washington, D.C.: U.S. Government Printing Office, 1978), pp. 101–12. See also U.S. Department of Housing and Urban Development, "A New Partnership to Conserve America's Communities," in *President's Urban and Regional Policy Group Report* (Washington, D.C.: U.S. Government Printing Office, 1978).

22. *Greater London Plan, 1944, a Report Prepared on Behalf of the Standing Conference on London Regional Planning by Professor Abercrombie* (London: HMSO, 1945); Ministry of Housing and Local Government, *The South-East Study, 1961–1981* (London: HMSO, 1964); South-East Economic Planning Council, *A Strategy for the South-East* (London: HMSO, 1967); South-East Joint Planning Team, *Strategic Plan for the South-East* (London: HMSO, 1970); Department of Environment, *Report of the Monitoring Group on Strategic Planning in the South-East* (London: HMSO, 1973); South-East Joint Planning Team, *Strategy for the South-East: 1976 Review* (London: HMSO, 1976).

23. See *Town and Country Planning* 49, no. 10 (Nov. 1980): 366–92, for new town and town development statistics.

24. Frank Schaffer, *The New Town Story* (London: Macgibbon and Kee, 1970).

25. H. Evans, ed. *New Towns: The British Experience* (London: Charles Knight, 1972); Ray Thomas, *London's New Towns: A Study of Self-Contained and Balanced Communities,* Broadsheet 510 (London: Political and Economic Planning, 1969).

26. *Report of the Commission on the Third London Airport* (London: HMSO, 1971).

27. Peter Hall et. al., *The Containment of Urban England,* 2 vols. (London: George Allen & Unwin, 1973).

28. Self, *Metropolitan Planning,* pp. 35–46.

29. Basic documentation of Paris planning is provided by the Institut d'Aménagement et d'Urbanisme de la Région d'Ile-de-France (IAURIF), a service of the prefecture de la région. The latest major plan is the *Schéma directeur d'aménagement et d'urbanisme de la Région d'Ile de France* (Paris: IAURIF, 1976), hereafter cited as *Schéma directeur,* 1976. IAURIF also publishes much useful background information. For the earlier history of the Paris plans, see Hall, *World Cities,* pp. 70–86.

30. *Schéma directeur d'aménagement et d'urbanisme de la région Parisienne,* prepared by District de la Région de Paris (now Région d'Ile de France) (Paris, 1965). For motives behind the plan, see the chapter by the first

new regional prefect, Paul Delouvrier, in W. A. Robson and D. Regan, eds., *Great Cities of the World*, pp. 730–71.

31. James Rubenstein, *The French New Towns* (Baltimore: Johns Hopkins University Press, 1978).

32. Until 1975 the new towns were absorbing about a quarter of the population growth and a fifth of new industrial floor space in the Paris region; from 1971 to 1975 about 60,000 dwellings were built in the towns, as compared with the 25,000 a year intended by the 1965 plan. *(Schéma directeur, 1976, pp. 152–53.)*

33. For the scale and implications of this proposal, see Department of Trade, *Report of the Study Group on South-East Airports*, (London: HMSO, 1979). See also Peter Self, *Econocrats and the Policy Process: The Politics and Philosophy of Cost-Benefit Analysis* (London: Macmillan, 1975), chap. 7.

34. U.S. Commission, *Population and the American Future;* N. M. Hansen, *The Challenge of Urban Growth* (Lexington, Mass.: Lexington Books, 1975), pp. 19–37.

35. G. M. Neutze, *Economic Policy and the Size of Cities* (Canberra: Australian National University Press, 1965).

36. *Schéma directeur, 1976,* pp. 20–23. See also *Vers un nouvel équilibre Paris-Province?* (Paris: Institut National de la Statistique et des Etudes Economiques [INSEE], 1976), and other works published by INSEE.

37. For a general review see R. G. Healy and J. S. Rosenberg, *Land Use and the States* (Baltimore: Johns Hopkins University Press, 1979).

38. B. J. Frieden, *The Environmental Protection Hustle* (Cambridge, Mass.: M.I.T. Press, 1979).

39. For the history of planning in Australian cities, see L. Sandercock, *Cities for Sale* (Carlton, Victoria: Melbourne University Press, 1975). For a general review see G. M. Neutze, *Australian Urban Policy* (Hornsby N.S.W.: George Allan & Unwin, 1978), and R. S. Parker and P. N. Troy, eds. *The Politics of Urban Growth* (Canberra: Australian National University Press, 1972).

40. Neutze, *Australian Urban Policy,* pp. 225–29.

41. For the planning history of South Australia, see Hugh Stretton, *Ideas for Australian Cities* (Melbourne: Georgian House, 1970), chaps. 6 and 7.

42. For the land commissions see Patrick Troy, *A Fair Price: The Land Commission Program, 1972–1977.* (Sydney: Hall & Iremonger, 1978). For departmental conflicts see Martin Painter and Bernard Carey, *Politics between Departments* (St. Lucia, Queensland: University of Queensland Press, 1979).

43. Richard Rose, ed. *The Management of Urban Change in Britain and Germany* (London: Sage Publications), pp. 171–85.

44. Derthick, *Between State and Nation,* chaps. 7–11. The federal regional councils cover large multistate areas that were standardized by President Nixon.

Chapter 5

1. J. O'Connor, *The Fiscal Crisis of the State* (London: St. James' Press, 1973).

2. T. A. Broadbent, *Planning, Profit, and the Urban Economy* (London: Methuen, 1977).

3. Peter Hall, *Great Planning Disasters* (London: Weidenfeld & Nicolson, 1980).

4. Hugh Stretton, *Capitalism, Socialism, and the Environment* (Cambridge: Cambridge University Press, 1976).

5. Fred Hirsch *Social Limits to Growth* (Cambridge, Mass.: Harvard University Press, 1976).

6. David Popenoe, *The Suburban Environment: Sweden and the United States* (Chicago: University of Chicago Press, 1977).

7. M. Castells, *The Urban Question* (London: Edward Arnold, 1977).

8. For the theories and practice of planning law, see Patrick McAuslan, *The Ideologies of Planning Law* (Oxford: Pergamon, 1980).

9. Robert Walker, *The Planning Function in Urban Government* (Chicago: University of Chicago Press, 1951).

10. R. Friedland, F. F. Piven, and R. R. Alford, "Political Conflict, Urban Structure, and the Fiscal Crisis," in *Comparing Public Policies,* ed. Douglas E. Ashford (Beverly Hills, Calif.: Sage Publications, 1978).

11. J. D. Stewart, *Management in Local Government: A Viewpoint* (London: Charles Knight, 1971).

12. Healy and Rosenberg, *Land Use and the States,* p. 242.

13. D. Mackay and A. Cox, *The Politics of Urban Change* (London: Croom Helm, 1979). For earlier history see Self, *Cities in Flood,* chap. 7.

14. For a general review see Neil Alison Roberts, ed., *The Government Land Developers* (Lexington, Mass.: Lexington Books, 1977).

15. E. P. Eichler and M. Kaplan, *The Community Builders* (Berkeley: University of California Press, 1967).

16. For regular reports see issues of *Town and Country Planning.*

17. Hall, *Strategic Planning in London.*

Bibliography

Altshuler, Alan A. *The City Planning Process: A Political Analysis.* Ithaca, N.Y.: Cornell University Press, 1965.

Anderson, Martin. *The Federal Bulldozer: A Critical Analysis of Urban Renewal, 1949–1962.* Cambridge, Mass.: M.I.T. Press, 1964.

Anton, T. J. *Governing Greater Stockholm.* Berkeley: University of California Press, 1975.

Ashford, Douglas E., ed. *Comparing Public Policies.* Beverly Hills, Calif.: Sage Publications, 1978.

Astrom, Kell. *City Planning in Sweden.* Stockholm: Swedish Institute, n.d.

Baldinger, Stanley. *Planning and Governing the Metropolis: The Twin Cities Experience.* New York: Praeger, 1971.

Banfield, E. C. *Political Influence.* Glencoe, Ill.: Free Press, 1961.

———. *The Unheavenly City.* Boston: Little, Brown, 1968.

Banfield, E. C., and Wilson, J. Q. *Urban Politics.* Cambridge, Mass.: Harvard University Press, 1963.

Berry, Brian J. L. *The Human Consequences of Urbanization.* London: Macmillan, 1973.

———, ed. *Urbanization and Counter-Urbanization.* Beverly Hills, Calif.: Sage Publications, 1976.

Bingham, R. D. *Public Housing and Urban Renewal.* New York: Praeger, 1975.

Bollens, J. C., and Schmandt, H. J. *The Metropolis.* New York: Harper & Row, 1970.

Broadbent, T. A. *Planning, Profit, and the Urban Economy.* London: Methuen, 1977.

Castells, M. *The Urban Question.* London: Edward Arnold, 1977.

Catanese, A. J. *Planners and Local Politics: Impossible Dreams.* Beverly Hills, Calif.: Sage Publications, 1974.

Clapp, J. A. *New Towns and Urban Policy.* New York: Dunellen, 1971.

Clark, Colin. *Population Growth and Land Use.* London: Macmillan, 1967.

Clawson, Marion, and Hall, Peter. *Planning and Urban Growth: An Anglo-American Comparison.* Baltimore, Md.: Johns Hopkins University Press, 1973.

Collins, M. F., and Pharoah, T. M. *Transport Organization in a Great City.* London: George Allen & Unwin, 1974.

Crecine, John P., ed. *Financing the Metropolis.* Beverly Hills, Calif.: Sage Publications, 1970.

Cullingworth, J. B. *Environmental Planning.* Vol. 3, *New Towns Policy.* London: H.M.S.O., 1979.

————. *Town and Country Planning in Britain.* London: George Allen & Unwin, 1974.

Dahl, R. A. *Who Governs? Democracy and Power in an American City.* New Haven: Yale University Press, 1961.

Danielson, Michael N., ed. *Metropolitan Politics: A Reader.* Boston: Little, Brown, 1966.

Delafons, John. *Land Use Controls in the United States.* Cambridge, Mass.: Harvard University Press, 1970.

Derthick, Martha. *Between State and Nation.* Washington, D.C.: Brookings Institution, 1974.

Donnison, D. *The Government of Housing.* London: Penguin, 1967.

Donnison, D., and Eversley, D., eds. *London: Urban Patterns, Problems, and Policies.* London: Heinemann, 1973.

Dunleavy, P. J. *The Politics of Mass Housing in Britain.* London: Oxford University Press, 1981.

Edwards, John, and Batley, Richard. *The Politics of Positive Discrimination: An Evaluation of the Urban Programme, 1967–77.* London: Tavistock Publications, 1978.

Eichler, Edward P., and Kaplan, Marshall. *The Community Builders.* Berkeley, University of California Press, 1967.

Elkin, S. *Politics and Land Use Planning: The London Experience.* London: Cambridge University Press, 1974.

Evans, H., ed. *New Towns: The British Experience.* London: Charles Knight, 1972.

Fishman, Robert. *Urban Utopias in the Twentieth Century: Ebenezer Howard, Frank Lloyd Wright, and Le Corbusier.* New York: Basic Books, 1977.

Foley, Donald L. *Governing the London Region.* Berkeley: University of California Press, 1972.

Frieden, B. J. *The Environmental Protection Hustle.* Cambridge, Mass.: M.I.T. Press, 1979.

Frieden, B. J., and Kaplan, Marshall. *The Politics of Neglect.* Cambridge, Mass.: M.I.T. Press, 1975.

Gans, Herbert. *The Levittowners: Ways of Life and Politics in a New Suburban Community.* New York: Pantheon, 1967.

————. *People and Plans.* New York: Basic Books, 1968.

Glasson, John. *An Introduction to Regional Planning.* London: Hutchinson, 1974.

Hall, P. *Great Planning Disasters.* London: Weidenfeld & Nicolson, 1980.

————. *Theory and Practice of Regional Planning.* London: Pemberton Books, 1970.

————. *The World Cities.* London: Weidenfeld & Nicolson, 1977.

Hall, P.; Thomas, Ray; Graley, Harry; and Drewett, Roy. *The Containment of Urban England.* 2 vols. London: George Allen & Unwin, 1973.

Hallam, Howard M. *Small and Large Together: Governing the Metropolis.* Berkeley, Calif.: Sage Publications, 1977.

Hambleton, Robin. *Policy Planning and Local Government.* London: Hutchinson, 1978.

Hancock, T., ed. *Growth and Change in the Future City Region.* London: Leonard Hill, 1976.

Hansen, N. M. *The Challenge of Urban Growth.* Lexington, Mass. Lexington Books, 1975.

———. *French Regional Planning.* Bloomington: Indiana University Press, 1968.

Harrigan, John J. *Political Change in the Metropolis.* Boston, Mass.: Little, Brown, 1976.

Hart, D. *Strategic Planning in London: The Rise and Fall of the Primary Road Network.* Oxford: Pergamon, 1976.

Harvey, David. *Social Justice and the City.* London: Edward Arnold, 1973.

Hayward, J., and Watson, M., eds. *Planning, Politics, and Public Policy.* Cambridge: Cambridge University Press, 1975.

Healy, R. G., and Rosenberg, J. S. *Land Use and the States.* Baltimore, Md.: Johns Hopkins University Press, 1979.

Heidenheimer, A. J., Heclo, H., and Adams, C. F. *Comparative Public Policy: The Politics of Social Choice in Europe and America.* London: Macmillan, 1976.

Hirsch, Fred. *Social Limits to Growth.* Cambridge, Mass: Harvard University Press, 1976.

Jacobs, Jane. *The Life and Death of Great American Cities.* London: Penguin, 1972.

Kaplan, Harold. *Urban Political Systems: A Functional Analysis of Metro Toronto.* New York: Columbia University Press, 1967.

Kramer, J., and Young, K. *Strategy and Conflict in Metropolitan Housing.* London: Heinemann, 1978.

Lagroye, J., and Wright, V., eds. *Local Government in Britain and France.* London: George Allen & Unwin, 1979.

Levin, P. H. *Government and the Planning Process.* London: George Allen & Unwin, 1976.

Lindblom, C. E. *The Policy Making Process.* Englewood Cliffs, N.J.: Prentice-Hall, 1968.

———. *Politics and Markets.* New York: Basic Books, 1977.

Maass, A., ed. *Area and Power.* Glencoe, Ill.: Free Press, 1959.

McAuslan, Patrick. *The Ideologies of Planning Law.* Oxford: Pergamon, 1980.

Mackay, D., and Cox, A. *The Politics of Urban Change.* London: Croom Helm, 1978.

Mathewson, Kent, ed. *The Regionalist Papers.* Southfield, Mich. Metropolitan Fund, 1978.

Merlin, Pierre. *New Towns.* London: Methuen, 1971.

Meyerson, M., and Banfield, E. *Politics, Planning, and the Public Interest.* Glencoe, Ill.: Free Press, 1964.

Mogulof, Melvin B. *Governing Metropolitan Areas: A Critical Review of Councils of Governments and the Federal Role.* Washington, D.C.: Urban Institute, 1971.

Moynihan, D. P. *Maximum Feasible Misunderstanding.* New York: Free Press, 1969.

Nelkin, Dorothy. *Jetport.* New Brunswick, N.J.: Transaction Books, 1974.

Neutze, G. M. *Australian Urban Policy.* Hornsby, N.S.W.: George Allen & Unwin, 1978.

————. *Economic Policy and the Size of Cities.* Canberra: Australian National University Press, 1965.

Osborn, F. J., and Whittick, A. *The New Towns.* New York: McGraw-Hill, 1963.

Parker, R. S., and Troy, P. N., eds. *The Politics of Urban Growth.* Canberra: Australian National University Press, 1972.

Pass, David. *Vällingby and Farsta—From Idea to Reality: The New Community Development in Stockholm.* Cambridge, Mass.: M.I.T. Press, 1973.

Peterson, Paul. *City Limits.* Chicago: University of Chicago Press, 1981.

Popenoe, David. *The Suburban Environment: Sweden and the United States.* Chicago: University of Chicago Press, 1977.

Pressman, Jeffrey L. *Federal Programs and City Politics: The Dynamics of the Aid Process in Oakland.* Berkeley: University of California Press, 1975.

Rabinovitz, Francine F. *City Politics and Planning.* New York: Atherton Press, 1969.

Rasmussen, S. E. *London, the Unique City.* 1936. Reprint. Cambridge, Mass.: M.I.T. Press, 1967.

Rhodes, Gerald. *The Government of London: The Struggle for Reform.* London: Weidenfeld & Nicolson, 1972.

————, ed. *The New Government of London: The First Five Years.* London: Weidenfeld & Nicolson, 1972.

Richards, Peter G. *The Reformed Local Government System.* London: George Allen & Unwin, 1975.

Roberts, Neil Alison, ed. *The Government Land Developers.* Lexington, Mass.: Lexington Books, 1977.

Robson, W. A., and Regan, D. E., eds. *Great Cities of the World.* London: George Allen & Unwin, 1972.

Rodwin, Lloyd. *Nations and Cities.* Boston: Houghton Mifflin, 1970.

Rondinelli, D. A. *Urban and Regional Planning.* Ithaca, N.Y.: Cornell University Press, 1975.

Rose, Albert. *Governing Metropolitan Toronto.* Berkeley: University of California Press, 1972.

Rose, Richard, ed. *The Management of Urban Change in Britain and Germany.* Beverly Hills, Calif.: Sage Publications, 1974.

Ross, G. and Cohen, S. *The Politics of French Regional Planning.* Baltimore, Md.: Johns Hopkins University Press, 1973.

Rubenstein, James. *The French New Towns.* Baltimore, Md.: Johns Hopkins University Press, 1978.

Sandercock, L. *Cities for Sale.* Carlton, Victoria: Melbourne University Press, 1975.

Schaffer, Frank. *The New Town Story.* London: Macgibbon and Kee, 1970.

Self, Peter. *Cities in Flood: The Problems of Urban Growth.* 2d ed. London: Faber & Faber, 1961.

———. *Econocrats and the Policy Process: The Politics and Philosophy of Cost-Benefit Analysis.* London: Macmillan, 1975.

———. *Metropolitan Planning: The Planning System of Greater London.* Greater London paper no. 14, London: London School of Economics, 1971.

Senior, Derek, ed. *The Regional City.* London: Longmans, Green, 1966.

Sharpe, L. J., ed. *Decentralist Trends in Western Europe.* Berkeley, Calif.: Sage Publications, 1979.

———. ed. *The Fiscal Crisis in West European Local Government: Myths and Realities.* London: Sage Publications, 1980.

Smallwood, Frank. *Greater London: The Politics of Metropolitan Reform.* New York: Bobbs-Merrill, 1965.

———. *Metro Toronto: A Decade Later.* Toronto: Bureau of Municipal Research, 1963.

Stewart, J. D. *Management in Local Government: A Viewpoint.* London: Charles Knight, 1971.

Stretton, Hugh. *Capitalism, Socialism, and the Environment.* Cambridge: Cambridge University Press, 1976.

———. *Ideas for Australian Cities.* Melbourne: Georgian House, 1970.

———. *Urban Planning in Rich and Poor Countries.* Oxford: Oxford University Press, 1978.

Sundquist, James. *Dispersing Population.* Washington, D.C.: Brookings Institution, 1975.

Thomson, J. M. *Great Cities and Their Traffic.* London: Penguin, 1978.

———. *Motorways in London.* London: Duckworth, 1969.

Troy, Patrick. *A Fair Price: The Land Commission Program 1972–1977.* Sydney: Hall & Iremonger, 1978.

Vickers, Sir Geoffrey. *The Art of Judgment.* London: Chapman and Hall, 1965.

Walker, Robert. *The Planning Function in Urban Government.* Chicago: University of Chicago Press, 1951.

Webber, M. M., *Explorations into Urban Structure.* Philadelphia: Pennsylvania University Press, 1964.

Wells, H. G. *Anticipations: The Reaction of Mechanical Progress on Human Life and Thought.* 1901. Reprint. London: Harper & Row, 1962.

Williams, Oliver P. *Metropolitan Political Analysis.* New York: Free Press, 1971.

Wilson, J. Q., ed. *Urban Renewal: The Record and the Controversy.* Cambridge, Mass.: M.I.T. Press, 1966.

Wood, Robert C. *1400 Governments.* Cambridge, Mass.: Harvard University Press, 1964.

Index